Bulletin
1975

Volume XXI

Los Angeles County Museum of Art

Bulletin 1975

Volume XXI

Los Angeles County Museum of Art

Published by the
Los Angeles County Museum of Art
5905 Wilshire Boulevard
Los Angeles, California 90036

Library of Congress
Catalog Card Number 58-35949

ISBN 0-87587-069-4
Printed in the United States of America

Cover
2.
Paolo Veronese
Old Man with Astrolabe
Oil on canvas
81 x 46 in. (206 x 117 cm.)
Los Angeles County Museum of Art
Gift of The Ahmanson Foundation

Frontispiece
Paolo Veronese
Old Man with Astrolabe (detail)
Oil on canvas
81 x 46 in. (206 x 117 cm.)
Los Angeles County Museum of Art
Gift of The Ahmanson Foundation

Designed in Los Angeles by
Evelyn Hirsch. All text set
in 9 Pt. Garamond by
Typographic Service Company,
Los Angeles. The catalog is printed
on Cameo by Color Graphics, Inc.
Los Angeles.

Contents

Two New Veroneses: The "Astronomers" at Los Angeles

Terisio Pignatti

The two so-called Astronomers that recently entered the collection of the Los Angeles County Museum of Art as a gift of the Ahmanson Foundation,[1] belong to what early writers defined as the "sublime manner" of the artist, that which he reserved especially for his most exacting and prestigious work (figs. 1, 2): figures fresh and immediate in treatment which preserve the fascination of the rapid and condensed touch of the "first idea"; astonishing in their colors, which vibrate mysteriously like precious materials; grandiose in their monumental compositions of foreshortened perspective and sophisticated scenographic effects.[2]

The history of the pictures is as singular and adventurous as their meaning is enigmatic. They appeared for the first time in 1881 in the exhibition of the Royal Academy of Arts in London,[3] lent by the Honorable Robert Baillie-Hamilton from his ancestral residence at Langton near Duns, Berwickshire. A perceptive reviewer took note of them in the *Atheneum* of January 8, judging them to be works of considerable importance.

It is presumed that Baillie-Hamilton had inherited the pictures through his wife from John Campbell, Marquess of Breadalbane, who had been a passionate collector of Italian pictures on his trips to the Continent in the 1830s. After the death of Robert Baillie-Hamilton, the paintings went to America to one of the fabulous villas in the "Belle Epoque" style in Newport, Rhode Island, owned by Robert Goelet. They remained unknown for a half century in the villa, which subsequently became Salve Regina College, where they were enclosed in pompous French frames, with their attribution changed from Veronese to Fragonard. They left there only in 1973 to be offered at auction at Sotheby's,[4] where they were purchased by Agnew's of London. I had the privilege of being one of the first to admire them in the studio of Mario Modestini in New York, where they then underwent a necessary but light restoration, essentially the removal of old obscuring varnish to give back to the colors the stunning brilliance that works in a perfect state of preservation have. The paintings were acquired from Agnew's by the Museum in 1974.

Rather enigmatic, as we have said, is the meaning of the paintings, one of which represents a bearded young man in a generically Renaissance costume, with an instrument in the form of a cross in his right hand, the other a bearded old man with a turban and dressed in a generically classical costume, with an anchor behind him and an astrolabe in his hands. Although separate, the two canvases show clearly their reciprocal relationship, if not otherwise than by their common architectural background of a high classical cornice that seems to enclose them both in a semicircle. Furthermore, both paintings share similar decorative elements, such as the sculptured cornice fragment and the Corinthian capital on which the figures lean. No matter how often they were identified as such in the past, they were obviously not patriarchs since it appeared evident that the "cross" held by the young man was not a religious object, but rather a special instrument, still to be identified; it was the astrolabe borne by the old man that eventually brought the interpretation into the sphere of astronomy. Two astronomers, then, or better yet, two allegories of navigation? This latter element, along with the evident iconological connection of the two canvases — to the point of raising the question whether they had not once been united in a single horizontal canvas — suggested the attractive hypothesis that they must have come from the Venetian palace of some famous navigator, or from one of the Magistracies of Waterways or from some room in the Arsenal. No indication of similar subjects, however, in the numerous lists of "lost pictures" by Veronese (that is, those cited by the early sources up to the eighteenth century, but whose location is presently unknown) could put us on the right track to an identification.

In the meantime, the research done by Clovis Whitfield of Agnew's in London, courteously sent to us, brought some light at least on the precise meaning of the instruments of the two "astronomers." The circular one, carried by the old man in the turban, is an astrolabe, the instrument used from ancient times to calculate the height of stars from the horizon. In common use everywhere in navigation, it was, according to tradition, invented by the Greeks at the time of Hipparchus, the astronomer who drew the first celestial map. The model in question, however, appears to be a typical Arab sixteenth-century instrument of inlaid ivory of the type called a "planispherion," that is, a flat astrolabe composed of a principal disc on which are superimposed numerous other small discs (up to nine) for the measurement of the stars. It seems to me that the temptation to identify the old man with Hipparchus himself, however, has to be rejected because of the turban, which seems rather to allude to an Arab. It was the Arabs, in fact, who, along with other nautical instruments, perfected the astrolabe to the extent that it remained in use until the adoption of the sextant in the eighteenth century. The object carried by the second "astronomer," made in the form of a cross, is actually another nautical instrument perfected by the Arabs in the late Middle Ages and in common use for navigation in the sixteenth century: a linear astrolabe called a cross-staff, an apparatus with measured crosspieces running along a longitudinal bar to measure, with the help of threads stretched between the extremities, the angles between the stars and the marine horizon.

We have then a confirmation that both the "astronomers" figure in the canvases not so much as scientists, but in the more practical role of navigators. The hypothesis of a "public" destination for the pictures, or in any case one

1.

3.

1.
Paolo Veronese (Italian, ca. 1528-1588)
Young Man with Cross-Staff
Oil on canvas
81 x 46 in. (206 x 117 cm.)
Los Angeles County Museum of Art
Gift of The Ahmanson Foundation

2.
Cover

3.
Attributed to Paolo Veronese
Young Man with Cross-Staff
Oil on canvas
57⅛ x 42⅛ in. (145 x 107 cm.)
Umtali, Southern Rhodesia
Collection of Stephen Courtauld

4.
Attributed to Paolo Veronese
Astronomer with Armillary Sphere
Oil on canvas
57⅛ x 42⅛ in. (145 x 107 cm.)
Umtali, Southern Rhodesia
Collection of Stephan Courtauld

4.

7.

8.

9.

7.
After Paolo Veronese
Young Man with Cross-Staff
Museum of Fine Arts, Chartres

8.
After Paolo Veronese
Old Man with Astrolabe
Museum of Fine Arts, Chartres

9.
After Paolo Veronese
Astronomer with Armillary Sphere
Museum of Fine Arts, Chartres

related to an ambience connected with navigation, is thus made altogether probable. And it is not without significance that the paintings were commissioned of Veronese in the epoch of the great geographic discoveries, in which navigators with exactly the instruments shown tackled the most adventurous courses.

It is interesting to recall, in conclusion, that two other figures identified as *Astronomer* and *Patriarch* are mentioned in the literature regarding Veronese:[5] canvases without doubt closely related to those in Los Angeles (figs. 3, 4). These are at present in the collection of the late Major Stephen Courtauld at Umtali in Southern Rhodesia, and were considered by Hendy in 1926, through Berenson in 1958, to be works of Veronese. While not knowing them *de visu,* it seems to me that one is a version in three-quarter length of the figure of the young astronomer with the cross-staff in Los Angeles. The other, however, shows an astronomer in Oriental costume, who has in his hand an armillary sphere, that is, a perfected model of a spherical astrolabe, which combines the planar astrolabe with the celestial globe and is a scientific instrument rather than one of practical use for navigation. The difference in measurement (57⅛ x 42⅛ inches as opposed to the 81 x 46 inches of the Los Angeles paintings, without excluding the possibility that this might have resulted from trimming) and the different background of the second Umtali painting, lacking all architectural elements, lead us to conclude that we are not dealing with a single group comprising the Umtali and Los Angeles paintings, but rather with a second, independent series.[6]

A final problem concerns the possible dating of the two canvases in Los Angeles. In my opinion, they belong to the period of Veronese's full maturity. In technique and style they are identical to the *Martyrdoms* in the presbytery of San Sebastiano in Venice, with which they share a fluid colorism, scintillating and luminescent, of broad, transparent, flowing layers of paint (figs. 5, 6). We are, therefore, between 1565 and 1570. Soon the personages with their vigorously expressive heads, characterized by strong and rapid brushstrokes, will appear in the great *Suppers* of the first years of the seventies, from Monte Berico to Venice, where the festive brilliance of the drapery will appear as frivolous and profane to the Tribunal of the Inquisition.

5.
Detail of fig. 1

6.
Paolo Veronese
Martyrdom of SS. Mark and Marcellian (detail)
Church of Saint Sebastian, Venice

This article is being published concurrently in Italian in the special issue of *Arte Veneta* (vol. 29, 1975) dedicated to Sergio Bettini on the occasion of his retirement from teaching at the University of Padua. Permission for the publication of an English translation by Kenneth Donahue has graciously been granted by the publisher and the author.

Terisio Pignatti, for many years director of the civic museums of Venice, is professor of History of Art at the University of Padua and the University of Venice. In 1966 he was visiting professor at the University of California, Berkeley. Professor Pignattti has organized and written the catalogs for a score of major exhibitions of Venetian painting and drawing in Italy, Germany, Austria, England, and the United States. He is distinguished internationally for his books on Carpaccio, Jacopo dei Barbari, Veronese, Canaletto, Tiepolo, and especially for his catalogues raisonnés of Pietro Longhi (1968), Giovanni Bellini (1969), and Giorgione (1969). His catalogue raisonné of Paolo Veronese is on the press for distribution in 1976.

5.
6.

Notes

1.
Kenneth Donahue illustrated them in color in *A Decade of Collecting, 1965–1975,* Los Angeles County Museum of Art, 1975, 174-75, plates 61, 62, generously leaving their publication to me.

2.
Old Man with Astrolabe; Young Man with Cross-Staff. Oil on canvas, each 81 x 46 in. (206 x 117 cm.). Inv. nos. M.74.99.1, M.74.99.2.

3.
London, Royal Academy of Arts, *Old Masters,* no. 164, young man called *Geometry and Navigation* and no. 166, old man called *Astronomy.*

4.
Sale catalog, *Important Old Master Paintings,* London, Sotheby, Dec. 12, 1973, no. 13, as *Astronomy* and *Patriarch.*

5.
Provenance: De Burlet, Bridgewater House, Agnew. Literature: P. Hendy, "Two Paintings by Paul Veronese," *Apollo,* Nov. 1926, 185-87; G. Fiocco, *Paolo Veronese,* Valori Plastici, Rome, 1934, 122, pl. LX a, b; B. Berenson, *Italian Pictures of the Renaissance, Venetian School* (London: Phaidon, 1957), vol. 1, 136; R. Marini and G. Piovene, *L'Opera completa del Veronese* (Milan: Rizzoli, 1968), no. 403.

6.
An interesting indication of Sylvie Beguin to Nicola Ivanoff (who cites it in his article "La Libreria Marciana" in the periodical *Saggi e Memorie di storia dell'arte,* VI, 1968, 78 n.) put us on the track of four paintings at the Museum of Fine Arts in Chartres which are closely related to the pictures presented here (figs. 7-9). They are in fact copies, apparently by a seventeenth-century hand, of the two Los Angeles "astronomers" and the Umtali Oriental astronomer with the armillary sphere, along with an allegory of sculpture which seems rather to be a copy after Zelotti. The Chartres copies were considered by Ivanoff as having come from the dispersed circle of paintings from the vestibule of the Marciana in Venice, described by G. Lorenzetti ("Di un disperso ciclo pittorico cinquecentesco nel Vestibolo della Libreria di San Marco," *Atti dell'Inst. Ven. di Sci. Lett. ed Arti,* 1942-43, 451). The present discovery, however, seems to exclude that possibility, not otherwise documented by Ivanoff.

1.

Lambert-Sigisbert Adam's "Bust of Neptune"

Peter Fusco
Associate Curator,
European Painting and Sculpture

With funds provided by the Michael J. Connell Foundation the Museum has recently been able to purchase an important terra-cotta bust of *Neptune*[1] (figs. 1-5) by the French sculptor Lambert-Sigisbert Adam (1700-1759).

One of the major sculptors at the court of Louis XV, Adam was also a leading exponent of French rococo sculpture, yet he has been little studied.[2] Along with much rococo art, his works experienced a relatively quick and complete fall from critical favor due to the development of a new, neo-classical taste in Europe around 1760.[3] Historically, Adam was cast as a loser because his career, but not his style, paralleled so closely that of Edme Bouchardon (1698-1762) – one of the initiators of neo-classicism in French sculpture. Also, Adam has been overshadowed by his more famous nephew, the virtuoso modeller of terra-cotta statuettes, Claude Michel, called Clodion (1738-1814).[4] Only recently, following a re-evaluation of baroque sculpture and Bernini (Adam's major source of inspiration), has Adam's place in the history of European sculpture been given serious scholarly attention.[5]

Relatively little is known of Adam's early career.[6] One of a family of sculptors,[7] he was born in Nancy and first trained by his father, Jacob-Sigisbert Adam. At the age of eighteen, in the winter of 1718-19, he worked at Metz, not far from his home town, and the following May his father sent him to Paris for further study. His Parisian masters are not known, but they were presumably French academicians.[8] In 1723, the French Royal Academy of Painting and Sculpture awarded Adam the *prix de Rome* for a relief representing *Evilmerodach Delivering Joachim from His Captivity.* This relief is now lost, and none of Adam's other early Parisian works have been recorded.

Adam left Paris in August 1723[9] and arrived in Rome on the 18th of September.[10] His first few years at the French Academy there were spent, along with fellow *pensionnaires,* studying the great works of antiquity and the revered masters such as Raphael.[11] During the year 1724 Adam executed models for a series of statues representing famous French kings and saints to be placed on the Spanish Steps;[12] but in 1725 this project was abandoned,[13] and the models for them have been lost or have yet to be identified.

Adam's earliest known surviving work is the Museum's bust of *Neptune.* Although it bears neither signature nor date, it can readily be identified as the terra-cotta model for a signed marble bust (fig. 6) in Schloss Charlottenburg, Berlin. Also at Charlottenburg is Adam's pendant marble bust of *Amphitrite* (fig. 7), the terra-cotta model for which is lost.[14] The date of these busts can be established fairly precisely. A *terminus ante quem* is provided by their mention in a letter of May 22, 1727, written by the director of the French Academy in Rome, Nicolas Wleughels:

Un des sculpteurs nommé Adam, qui est Lorrain, lui {the Cardinal de Polignac} fit voir deux bustes qu'il a travaillez, représentant une Amphitrite et un Neptune qu'il a faits par étude. Ces deux morceaux plurent si fort qu'il les a pris pour orner son appartement; . . .[15]

Since the marble busts in Charlottenburg are those which appear in inventories of Polignac's collection,[16] one may safely assume that they, and not the terra-cotta models, are the works the Cardinal "a pris pour orner son appartement" in May 1727. The Museum's bust, as well as a lost terra-cotta model for the *Amphitrite,* must have been made at some point prior to the marbles; undoubtedly the models were themselves preceded by preliminary clay sketches or drawings. There is, in fact, evidence to suggest that Adam's first studies for these busts were done nearly two years before Polignac acquired the marbles: Dézallier d'Argenville, in his life of Adam, refers to "les bustes de Neptune & Amphitrite qu'il avoit faits pour son étude, deux ans après son arrivée en Italie,"[17] which would place Adam at work on the busts during the end of 1725. Thus, it is probable that the Museum's *Neptune* was executed at some point between late 1725 and May of 1727 when the finished marbles were taken to decorate Polignac's residence.

Cardinal Melchior de Polignac (1661-1741) had been in Rome since April 1724, and in August of that year was appointed French *chargé d'affaires* or acting ambassador to the Holy See.[18] As the highest ranking official of the French government in Rome, and encouraged by his passion for the arts, he quite naturally became the protector of the French Academy in Rome. His contact with Adam was to be expected. Polignac would certainly have known Adam's 1724 models for the statues projected for the Spanish Steps. Also, in July 1726, it was through Polignac's intercession that Adam obtained permission to copy the famous *Ludovisi Mars.*[19] Moreover, the cardinal was a constant guest at the French Academy and he frequently visited the studios of the young artists. It was on one of these occasions that he saw, apparently for the first time, and decided to purchase the marble busts of *Neptune* and *Amphitrite.*

One puzzling point should be mentioned. Both Wleughels and d'Argenville, in the passages cited above, seem to indicate that Adam not only began work on the two mythological busts as studies, but that he also executed the final marbles "par étude" before Polignac came to know of them. It is tempting to disregard this interpretation as a false reading of imprecise documents, since it would have been rather unusual for even an established sculptor, let alone a student, to carve expensive marble without first securing a patron to purchase the material and pay for the work. Yet the only other eighteenth-century account of these busts, the reliable biography of Adam by Dom Calmet, also suggests the same sequence of events:

Adam étant encore Pensionnaire du Roy à Rome, fit

2.

3.

1-5.
Lambert-Sigisbert Adam
(French, 1700-1759)
Neptune, 1725-1727
Terra cotta
Height including socle:
30¾ in. (80.6 cm.)
Height without socle:
27 in. (68.6 cm.)
Los Angeles County Museum of Art
Gift of the
Michael J. Connell Foundation
M. 75.70

5.

4.

deux Bustes en marbre de sa composition, représentant Neptune & Amphitrite; . . . il avoit fait ces deux Bustes par étude; M. le Cardinal de Polignac les ayant vus, les lui acheta. . . .[20]

Certain events in Adam's later career lend credence to the idea that he would have carved marble busts without a commission. For example, early in 1733 Adam donated to the Roman *Accademia di San Luca* an elaborate marble bust representing *Dolore*[21] (an allegory of grief); this was one of the rare, because uncalled for, instances of a marble rather than terra-cotta *morceau de reception* being given to the Roman academy. Also, during the 1740s Adam — again, apparently, without a commission — carved a large marble bust of Louis XV,[22] which remained unsold at the artist's death. From all indications Adam was aggressively ambitious throughout his career, and this aspect of his personality may have had a part in the creation of the *Neptune* and *Amphitrite* busts. In fact, a cynical historian might recall that while Adam was in Rome there remained one outstanding area at Versailles — the *Bassin de Neptune* — that clearly still needed sculptural decoration; and Adam may have undertaken his uncommissioned marble busts precisely in order to show off with subjects appropriate for that forthcoming project. Eventually, upon his return to France, Adam received this commission and executed a colossal lead group, *The Triumph of Neptune and Amphitrite* (fig. 8),[23] for Versailles.

As a type within the history of sculpture, non-portrait busts, such as the *Neptune* and *Amphitrite*, have received little study.[24] More often than not, busts of mythological and allegorical figures seem to have been marginal works insofar as they were created either as decorative adjuncts to a given architectural setting or as spin-offs from full figures. However, while in Rome, Adam made something of a specialty of this genre of sculpture. In addition to the *Neptune* and *Amphitrite*, as well as the bust of *Dolore* mentioned above, he also executed pendant busts of *Achilles* and *Ulysses* and a series of four busts of the elements *Fire, Earth, Wind* and *Water*.[25] This concentration upon the non-portrait bust per se undoubtedly stemmed from Adam's own basically decorative inclinations. However, it may also be considered a reflection of a more general tendency of the period: the focusing on and rise in prestige of what had previously been considered minor or decorative art forms.

The Museum's *Neptune* is of particular interest since it is one of only three known terra cottas by Adam.[26] The subtlety of modeling in areas such as the chest and forehead, and the crispness of detail in the beard and eyes — with the audacious scooping out of the pupils — indicate a technical mastery which is startling for an artist in his mid-twenties. Inspection of the bust from above shows that the head was first modeled more or less "bald," and that the cattails and reeds were made separately, then

6.

7.

6.
Lambert-Sigisbert Adam
Neptune, ca. 1727
Marble
Height without socle:
27⅛ in. (69 cm.)
Schloss Charlottenburg, Berlin

7.
Lambert-Sigisbert Adam
Amphitrite, ca. 1727
Marble
Height without socle:
21⅝ in. (55 cm.)
Schloss Charlottenburg, Berlin

placed on top while the clay was still damp. This additive working method and the general overall virtuosity of handling display a hitherto unknown dimension of Adam's talents (he has always been recognized as an extraordinary marble carver) and provide an insight into the kind of training that lies behind the renowned terra cottas of Adam's nephew and pupil, Clodion.

A comparison of the Charlottenburg marble *Neptune* with the Museum's bust (figs. 1 and 6) reveals numerous compositional differences. In the marble the head is turned more sharply to the left, and the large drapery clasp has been moved from the center of the chest over to the left and back slightly into the crevice between the chest and left upper arm. Along with these changes, the marble has become narrower, from front to back, than the terra cotta. The drapery sweeps upward and outward on the left side of the terra cotta as we look at it; in the marble the cloak's outward movement has been curtailed, rising up around the shoulder in a more strictly vertical line. These changes may all be concessions to the limits of the marble block.

Not only is the head more sharply turned in the marble, but it is also slightly raised and, as if to compensate for this, part of the beard drops further down upon the chest. With the tilting of the head, the general conception of Neptune has been altered. The marble conveys a fiercer, more outward looking and resolute, but also more conventional, image of the sea god; in contrast, the lowered head of the terra cotta evokes a more introspective figure. There is a gentleness created by the graceful curvilinear rhythms of the terra cotta's beard and drapery, while in the marble, with its more angular rhythms, there is a sense of tensed readiness. The subtle modeling of the chest in the terra cotta, clearly depicting the softness of an old man's flesh, adds an element of vulnerability which is especially unusual in the portrayal of Neptune.

After his return to France in 1733 Adam was to treat the subject of Neptune in two other important works: the large lead group at Versailles (referred to above, fig. 8) and the figure of *Neptune Calming the Waves* (fig. 9), executed as a *morceau de reception* for the French Academy in 1737 and now in the Louvre. The head of the Louvre figure follows quite closely, in physiognomy and feeling, the marble bust at Charlottenburg (compare figs. 12 and 6). However, the lead *Neptune* at Versailles (fig. 10) shows a marked transformation[27] to a more brutally forceful head with very bushy eyebrows and thicker, grosser features — a type that would seem to have been inspired by the head of Bernini's famous *Neptune and Triton* (fig. 11).[28] In contrast, it is notable that in his earlier depiction of Neptune, the Museum's bust, Adam is not so much influenced by Bernini as by one of the renowned Renaissance sculptures in Rome, the *Moses* of Michelangelo (compare figs. 13 and 14). The drooping

9.

8.
Lambert-Sigisbert Adam
French, 1700-1759
The Triumph of Neptune and Amphitrite, 1736-1740
Lead
Over life-size
Bassin de Neptune, Versailles

9.
Lambert-Sigisbert Adam
Neptune Calming the Waves, 1737
Marble
Height: 33⅞ in. (86 cm.)
Musée du Louvre, Paris

10.
Detail of fig. 8

11.
Gian Lorenzo Bernini
(Italian, 1598-1680)
Neptune and Triton (detail), 1620
Marble
Over life-size
Victoria and Albert Museum, London

8.

10.

11.

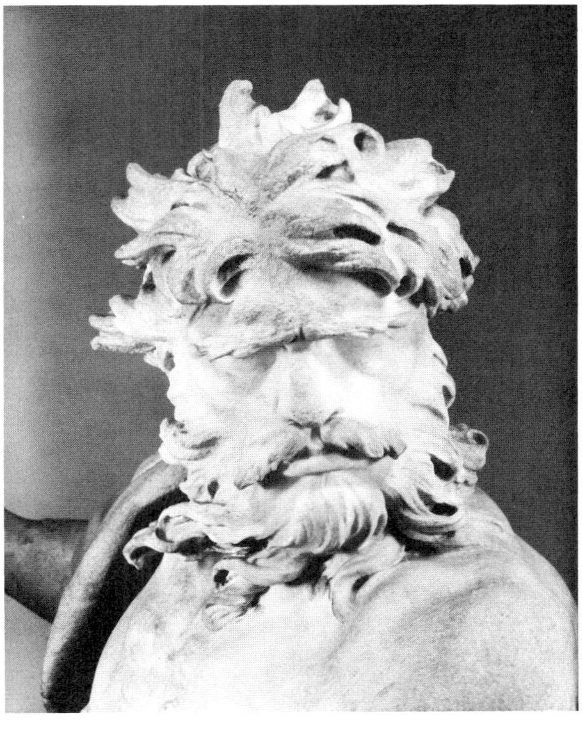

12.

moustache, flowing beard, and knitted brows of the *Moses* would certainly seem to be the sources for similar elements in Adam's terra cotta, and it is even tempting to see the cattails on *Neptune's* head as a kind of secular transformation of *Moses'* horns. Although he was most constantly influenced by Bernini in his later career, it is perhaps not surprising that when Adam first arrived in Rome he turned for inspiration to the greatest Renaissance sculptor.

Adam's bust of *Neptune* was apparently always intended to represent the ruler of the seas and has always been referred to as such, but the reeds and cattails in the hair are more commonly the attributes of a river god.[29] Out of these attributes Adam fashioned a playful crown which, together with the decorative clasps[30] and the elegant flow of beard and drapery, produces a lightness and graceful animation that cushion the serious face adopted from Michelangelo. This lightness in tone, employed in the treatment of a traditionally heroic subject, is one of the reasons Adam's works were condemned at the end of the eighteenth century. When it was created, however, the bust of *Neptune* was an innovative work, one of the earliest examples of the new rococo style.

13.

14.

12.
Detail of fig. 9

13.
Detail of fig. 1

14.
Michelangelo (Italian, 1475-1564)
Moses (detail), 1513-1516
Marble
Over life-size
San Pietro in Vincoli, Rome

Postscript

One of Adam's greatest triumphs came in Rome in 1731, when he won a competition held by Clement XII for designs to build the Trevi Fountain.[31] Eventually, for chauvinistic reasons, the fountain was erected by Italian artists, and Adam's winning model for the fountain is now lost. However, an early detailed description of the model[32] states that two of its major figures were a reclining male representing *Oceanus* on one side, and, on the other, a reclining female figure of *The Mediterranean.* It seems probable that Adam's busts of *Neptune* and *Amphitrite*, executed only a few years earlier, provide images that are very close to the two figures from his lost fountain model.

Appendix

Biography of Lambert-Sigisbert Adam in Niccolo Gabburri's manuscript *vite* in the Biblioteca Nazionale Centrale, Florence (Mss. Palat., E.B.9.5., volume III, page 1737, aggiunti alla lettera L, written between 1734 and 1737):

Lamberto Sigisberto Adam, nativo di Nansy in Lorena, scultore di Luigi 15° Re' di Francia studiò in Roma nell'Accademia Reale per lo spazio di 9 anni, nel qual tempo seriamente applicando, fece maraviglioso profitto, come ne fanno ampia testimonianza alcune opere di scultura fatte da Esso e lasciate in Roma. Fra quelle merita special menziona un bellissimo Busto di Marmo di un vecchio figurato per il Dolore donato da Esso all'Accademia di S.° Luca di Roma per dimostrare il dolore intenso che Egli provava nel doversi partire da quella sua diletta Città. Ha fatto parimente un Bassorilievo in Marmo, istoriato per l'Eccelentissima casa Corsini, esprimendo quando Sant Andrea Corsini riceve il Pastorale. Terminato appena il detto Bassorilievo, che fù nell'anno 1733; e della sua età di anni 32, venne richiamato in Francia da quel Ré, e fu dichiarato Scultore di S. M. Nel suo ritorno in Francia passando per la Città di Firenze si tratenne (?) in Essa qualche tempo con sua gran piacere a ragione del gran numero delle bellissime statue che qui vi osservò dicendo, che in genere di scultura, la Città di Firenze, toltané Roma, era la meglio fornita e la più deliziosa di tutte. / Sentimento totalmente opposto, ma però, veridico a ciò che scrive Luigi Scaramuccia nel suo Girupeno./[33] *Vive ora questo virtuoso, e degno Professore in Parigi, adorno di gentilezza, e di ottimi costumi, occupato sempre in grandiose opere di Scultura per quella R. M.à la quale subito, che Egli giunge in Parigi, lo dichiarò suo Scultore Regio e gli assegnò quatiere e studio nel Palazzo Reale del Louvre. Fu Scritto al catologo degli Accademici di S. Luca di Roma, e trovasi registrato il suo nome nel Libro intitolato "Gli Eccelsi Pregi delle Belle Arti" impresso in Roma nel 1733 in fine. Fu ascritto per uno degli Accademici di onore nell' Accad.ª Clementina di Bologna, come scrive Gianpietro Zannotti, nella sua storia di dª Accad.ª Libro 4° a 334.*[34]

Notes

1.
When acquired, the bust was covered with a thin wash of pigment applied at a relatively recent date; this wash has now been removed. Beneath the wash were traces of greenish and reddish non-aqueous media which together formed a brown-black color (seeming to indicate that the terra cotta was once painted to look like a bronze—a common practice in the late eighteenth and nineteenth centuries). These traces of red and green have also been removed. The terra cotta contains a number of firing cracks (a normal occurrence in the baking of a large clay model). At an unknown date these cracks were crudely and unnecessarily restored with putty luting; the Museum's conservators have removed as much as was safely possible of the crude restorations on the front of the bust. An equally crude filling in the cavity at the lower back has been left intact since it is not visible and provides extra support at the point where the bust is mounted on its socle. In general, the bust is in excellent condition for such a large terra cotta with numerous projecting elements. Only the original tips of the cattails, on top of the head, are lacking; these have been restored. A piece of one of the reeds, also on the head, was at one time broken off, but was retained and fixed in place by an earlier restorer. The surface of the bust has, in a number of places, tiny pits which are the result of air bubbles bursting when the clay was originally fired. Credit for the careful technical study, cleaning and restoration of the bust is due to the Museum's conservators Peter Dammers, Ben Johnson, and Billie Millam.

2.
The most important early source of information about Adam is Dom Calmet, *Bibliothèque Lorraine ou histoire des hommes illustres qui ont fleuri en Lorraine . . .*, Nancy, 1751, columns 9-16; Calmet's biography is based upon information supplied by L.-S. Adam's brother, Nicolas-Sebastien Adam. An earlier, much briefer life of L.-S. Adam is to be found in Niccolo Gabburri's manuscript *vite* in the Biblioteca Nazionale Centrale, Florence; this is published for the first time as an appendix to the present article. The other major eighteenth-century biography of Adam appears in A.-N. Dézallier d'Argenville's *Vies des fameux sculpteurs depuis la renaissance des arts avec la description de leurs ouvrages*, Paris, 1787, vol. 2, pp. 339-52; for the most part d'Argenville's biography of Adam is based upon Dom Calmet. For more recent literature on Adam see the following notes.

3.
For typical late eighteenth-century criticism of Adam's style, see C.-H. Watelet and P.-C. Lévesque, *Dictionnaire des arts de peinture, sculpture, et gravure*, Paris, 1792, vol. 1, 456; P. Chennevières and A. de Montaiglon, eds., "Abecedario de P. J. Mariette," *Archives de l'art français*, vol. 2, 1851-53, 7-8; P. L., "Jugements de Bachaumont sur les meilleurs artistes de son temps," *Revue universelle des arts*, vol. 5, 1857, 420.

4.
Even the most extensive study of Adam (H. Thirion, *Les Adam et Clodion*, Paris, 1885) is primarily concerned with providing a biographical background for Clodion. The same is true of A. Jacquot, *Les Adam et les Michel et Clodion*, Paris, 1898.

5.
See T. Hodgkinson, "A Bust of Louis XV by L.-S. Adam," *Burlington Magazine*, vol. 94, 1952, 36-40 (the attribution made therein was later discarded by Hodgkinson, *Victoria and Albert Museum Yearbook*, London, 1972, no. 3, 114, note 1); A. Arfelli, "Due lettere dello scultore lorenese Lambert Sigisbert Adam," *L'Archiginnasio* (Bolletino della Biblioteca Communale di Bologna), vol. 40, 1965, 438-45; P. Pradel, "La place des sculpteurs Lambert et Nicolas Adam dans la sculpture française au XVIIIe siècle," *La Lorraine dans l'Europe des lumières*, Nancy, 1968, 343-47; M. Levey, *Art and Architecture of the Eighteenth Century in France*, Hammondsworth/Baltimore, 1972, 63-67; F. Souchal, "Inventaire après decès du sculpteur Lambert-Sigisbert Adam," *Bulletin de la Société de l'Histoire de l'Art Français*, Année 1973, Paris, 1974, 181-91. The most useful list of L.-S. Adam's works is still S. Lami, *Dictionnaire des sculpteurs de l'ècole française au dix-huitième siècle*, Paris, 1910, vol. 1, 2-9.

6.
Calmet, *Bibliothèque Lorraine*, col. 9, provides the few scanty facts known about Adam's early career.

7.
In addition to his father Jacob-Sigisbert (1670-1747), his two younger brothers, Nicolas-Sebastien (1705-1778) and François-Gaspard-Balthasar (1710-1761), were also sculptors.

8.
Lami, *Dictionnaire*, 2, suggested that Adam had worked in the studio of François Dumont; F. Souchal, "François Dumont, sculpteur de transition (1688-1726)," *Gazette des Beaux-Arts*, vol. 75, 1970, 225-50, has also proposed that Adam was influenced by Dumont. For circumstantial as well as stylistic reasons, it seems probable that Dumont was one of the "differens habiles sculpteurs" under whom, according to Calmet, *Bibliothèque Lorraine*, col. 9, Adam was trained during his early years in Paris.

9.
Ibid.

10.
A. de Montaiglon, *Correspondance des directeurs de l'académie de France à Rome avec les surintendants des bâtiments,* Paris, 1857-1908, vol. 6, 285.

11.
Ibid., vol. 6, 304, 340.

12.
Ibid., vol. 6, 322, 328, 334-35, 341, 455-56; vol. 7, 7-8, 15-17, 29, 35, 43, 85-86. Bouchardon and Pierre Lestache also did models for this series of statues.

13.
This change of plans may have resulted from the appointment, in August 1724, of the Cardinal de Polignac as a new French minister in Rome; see Ibid., vol 7, 84-85. It seems less likely (as has been suggested by A. Roserot, "La vie et l'oeuvre d'Edme Bouchardon en Italie," *Gazette des Beaux-Arts,* vol. 40, 1908, 18) that is was Nicolas Wleughels who initiated the change in plans; however, after Wleughels assumed the directorship of the French Academy in Rome in September 1725, his first recorded remarks on the projected statues (Montaiglon, *Correspondance,* vol. 7, 232) reveal a negative attitude toward them. For the history of the Spanish Steps see especially W. Lotz, "Die spanische Treppe. Architektur als Mittel der Diplomatie," *Römische Jahrbuch für Kunstgeschichte,* vol. 12, 1969, 39-94, with further literature.

14.
The Charlottenburg *Neptune* and *Amphitrite* measure, respectively, 27⅛ in. (69 cm.) and 21⅝ in. (55 cm.) high, without their socles. The *Neptune* is signed: *Lem^{t}. Sigisbert Adam in. et fec.;* the *Amphitrite* is unsigned. I would like to thank Dr. Helmut Börsch-Supan, Museumdirektor, Schloss Charlottenburg, for his help in obtaining photographs of these busts. On the provenance of the marbles, see note 16.

15.
"One of the sculptors named Adam, who is from Lorrain, showed him [the Cardinal de Polignac] two busts that he worked, representing an Amphitrite and a Neptune which he made for study. These two pieces pleased so much that he took them to decorate his apartment. . . . " Montaiglon, *Correspondance,* vol 7, 348. This letter was first cited by Thirion, *Les Adam et Clodion,* 38, who incorrectly dated it 1724, thus implying that the marbles were done at that time; following Thirion, Lami, *Dictionnaire,* 4, and Levey, *Art and Architecture,* 64, have also dated the Charlottenburg marbles to 1724.

16.
See J. Guffrey, "Inventaire du mobilier et des collections antiques et modernes du Cardinal de Polignac 1738," *Nouvelles archives de l'art français,* 3rd ser., vol. 15, 1899, 252-97, items 594 and 595. Also see the sale catalog following Polignac's death: *Etat et description des statues, tant colossales que de grandeur naturelle et de demie nature, bustes grands, moyens et demi-bustes, bas-reliefs de différentes espèces, urnes, colonnes, inscriptions et autres ouvrages antiques, tant grecs que romains, trouvés à Rome; assemblés et apportés en France par feu M. le Cardinal de Polignac,* Paris, 1742, items 227 and 228. Polignac's collection of sculpture was purchased by Frederick the Great, via his Parisian agent Mathieu François Petit, on July 17, 1742; for the sale contract see M. Rambaud, *Documents du minutier central concernant l'histoire de l'art, vol. I* (1700-1750), Paris, n.d. [1964], 708-709. The busts were placed by Frederick in his chateau Sanssouci at Potsdam, where they are mentioned by Matthieu Oesterrich, *Description de tout l'interieur des deux palais de Sans-Souci de ceux de Potsdam, et de Charlottenburg . . . ,* Potsdam, 1773, 83, items 9 and 10. The busts remained at Sanssouci until at least 1900 (see P. Seidel, *Les collections d'oeuvres d'art français du XVIIIe siècle, appartenant à sa majesté l'empereur d'allemagne roi de Prusse,* Berlin/Leipzig, 1900, cat. nos. 172 and 173) but were moved to Charlottenburg before World War II.

17.
"the busts of Neptune and Amphitrite that he had made for his study, two years after his arrival in Italy." D'Argenville, *Vies des fameux sculpteurs,* 340.

18.
On Polignac see A. Jacotin, *Preuves de la maison de Polignac,* Paris, 1905, and P. Paul, *Le Cardinal Melchoir de Polignac (1661-1741),* Paris, 1922. For some of the Cardinal's activities as an art patron, see also C. Juge-Chapsal, "Le Cardinal de Polignac, Mecène, son portrait au pastel par Rosalba Carriera," *L'Auvergne litteraire,* 1956, 9-20, and M. Levey, "Panini, St. Peter's and Cardinal de Polignac," *Burlington Magazine,* vol. 99, 1957, 53-54.

19.
Montaiglon, *Correspondance,* vol. 7, 258, 273. Executed between 1726 and 1730 for Louis XV, Adam's copy of the *Ludovisi Mars* was later given by the French king to Frederick the Great; it arrived in Potsdam in 1752 and is today still in the chateau Sanssouci. See Thirion, *Les Adam et Clodion,* 43-44; Lami, *Dictionnaire,* 4; M. Furcy-Raynaud, "Inventaire des sculptures executées au XVIIIe siècle," *Archives de l'art français,* vol. 14, 1927, 421ff.

20.
"Adam being still a pensioner of the King in Rome, made two busts in marble of his composition, representing Neptune & Amphitrite; . . . he had made these two busts for study; the Cardinal de Polignac having seen them, bought them from him. . . . " Calmet, *Bibliothèque Lorraine,* col. 13.

21.
See Lami, *Dictionnaire,* 5; Riccoboni, *Roma nell'arte,* Rome, 1942, 305; *Il settecento a Roma,* ex. cat., Rome, 1959, p. 41.

22.
See Hodgkinson, *Burlington Magazine* 1952, passim.

23.
See Furcy-Raynaud, *Inventaire,* 2ff.

24.
Although they do not represent mythological figures, Bernini's *Anima Beata* and *Anima Dannata* (see R. Wittkower, *Gian Lorenzo Bernini,* 2nd ed., London, 1966, cat. no. 7) are the major typological precedents, if not the direct sources, for Adam's pendant non-portrait busts. Pendant busts of *Neptune* and *Amphitrite,* attributed to an unknown Dutch sculptor of the early eighteenth century, are in the Rijksmuseum (see J. Leeuwenberg and W. Halsema-Kubes, *Beeldhouwkunst in het Rijksmuseum,* Amsterdam, 1973, cat. nos. 363a-b). Adam's *Neptune* and *Amphitrite* were undoubtedly influential upon the pendant busts of *Chryses* and *Iphigenia* by Michel-Ange Slodtz (see F. Souchal, *Les Slodtz, sculpteurs et decorateurs du Roi, 1685-1764,* Paris, 1967, pp. 198-99, 658-59). In general, busts of mythological and allegorical figures seem to have become more commonplace toward the end of the seventeenth and beginning of the eighteenth century, paralleling the growth in importance of portrait busts.

25.
For proof that the latter six busts were executed in Rome see Souchal, *Inventaire après decès,* 184. nos. 47-48 and p. 186, nos. 76-79. After his death, Adam's busts of the four elements evidently went to Russia where bronze casts of them were made in the 1780s (cf. *Khudozhestvennyia sokrovischa Rossii,* vol. I, 1905, pls. 7-8 and accompanying, unpaginated, text); a fragment of the terra-cotta model for the bust of *Water* is in the Hermitage (see Z. Zaretskay and N. Kosseréva, *La sculpture française des XVII-XX siècles au Musée de l'Ermitage,* Leningrad, 1963, pls. 18-19).

26.
The other two are the fragment (mentioned in the preceding note) and the relief of *The Virgin Appearing to Saint Andrea Corsini* in the Musée des Beaux-Arts, Nancy (see "Musée de Nancy, un bas-relief de L.-S. Adam," *Beaux Arts,* vol. 3, 1925, 328; A. E. Brinckmann, *Barock-Bozzetti,* Frankfurt-am-Main, 1925, vol. 3, 100-101; H. Roy, "Un bas-relief de Sigisbert Adam," *Bulletin artistique de l'est,* vol. 25, 1926, no. 3, 7-8).

27.
This change may be due in part to the lead *Neptune's* location which required it to be seen from a great distance.

28.
The overall composition of Adam's *Neptune Calming the Waves* (fig. 9), but not its head, is also based closely upon Bernini's *Neptune and Triton.*

29.
See, for example, V. Cartari, *Imagini delli dei de gl'antichi,* Venice, 1647, pp. 129ff.

30.
The use of large decorative clasps to punctuate the drapery design in both the *Neptune* and the *Amphitrite* is a device which Adam may have adopted from Bernardino Cametti; compare Cametti's statue of *Diana* (U. Schlegel, "Bernardino Cametti," *Jahrbuch der Berliner Museen,* vol. 5, 1963, 151ff, figs. 38-40), the face of which is also very similar to that of Adam's *Amphitrite.* It should be noted that the use of large drapery clasps goes back to antique busts and was first revived by Michelangelo in his *Brutus* (see C. De Tolnay, *Michelangelo,* Princeton, 1954, vol. 4, 76ff); also, the *Brutus,* insofar as its sharp turn of the head and glowering features are concerned, is an early predecessor of Adam's bust of *Neptune.*

31.
Most recently on the Trevi Fountain see H. L. Cooke, Jr., "The Documents Relating to the Fountain of Trevi," *Art Bulletin,* vol. 38, 1956, 149-73; A. Schiavo, *La Fontana di Trevi e le altre opere di Nicola Salvi,* Rome, 1956; C. D'Onofrio, *Le Fontane di Roma,* Rome, 1957, pp. 225-70; M. Rotili, "I Progetti di Luigi Vanvitelli per la Fontana di Trevi," *Studi Romani,* vol. 21, no. 3, 1973, 314-331. Despite this literature and earlier writings on the fountain, we still lack a full and satisfactory account of the fountain competitions under Clement XII.

32.
Calmet, *Bibliothèque Lorraine,* columns 9-10.

33.
Luigi Scaramuccia, *Le finezze de pennelli italiani, ammirate, e studiate da Girupeno sotta la scorta, e disciplina del genio di Raffaello d'Urbino . . . ,* Pavia, 1674.

34.
Gian Pietro Zanotti, *Storia dell'Accademia Clementina,* Bologna, 1739, vol. 2, 334.

1.

An Unknown Early Work by Ignaz Günther: "St. Scholastica"

Gerhardt P. Woeckel

The discovery a few years ago of a Mary Immaculate (fig. 2), an early work of about 1752-53 by Ignaz Günther, in the remote town of Kopřivnà-Geppersdorf in the Moravian Altvater Mountains of Czechoslovakia caused an art historical sensation of major importance.[1] Articles by Karl Sitzman (1951),[2] Heinrich Decker (1953),[3] and by this writer (1954 and 1967)[4] have already provided quite a precise idea of Günther's works known to date and the present publication of another previously unknown piece, the St. Scholastica (fig. 1)* will help further our knowledge. We assume that this figure probably dates to the years around 1754, the beginning of his early period, when the artist returned to Munich. Since only a few of his early works have been preserved, compared to the greater number extant from his later period of production, our knowledge of Günther's beginnings as an artist has been limited. The subject of our discussion is a figure carved of linden wood (130 cm. high, with crozier 158 cm.) representing St. Scholastica.[5] Its assumed provenance, characteristic attributes, religious habit, and particular iconographic and stylistic problems will be discussed later.

Although it is not important at this point to analyze the entire composition in detail, we should note the steep isosceles triangle that is the formal basis of the entire composition, for this is one of Günther's favorite stylistic devices, as I have pointed out elsewhere. The use of a directional line that visually cuts through the figure from the book on the right to the sphere on the lower left shows how carefully the formal structure of this figure had been studied. The figure is in a perfect state of conservation. The light grayish bole ground that originally served as a foundation for the surface color is totally preserved, and the light skin tone of the face and hands is of the same period. The gold leaf covering the red bole ground of the head of the crozier and the sphere at the base is also original.

St. Scholastica is represented wearing the customary nun's habit over a narrow-sleeved garment. The abundant robe with wide sleeves is typical. She is thus identified not only "as a nun of a religious order, but in particular as a Benedictine," according to J. Braun.[6] She wears a veil and a wimple, a cloth that covers her neck and the upper part of her shoulders. Contrary to the general rule, the coif, a close-fitting head covering, is missing from this representation. Originally the wimple must have been white and would have made a striking contrast to the veil, which we assume must have been black, the color of the habit of the order. With the exception of the missing coif, the habit depicted in this sculpture corresponds exactly to the one introduced in 1603 into the order "of the reformed Benedictine Nuns of Our Lady of Peace." The most striking attribute of the figure is the crozier with its richly carved head, which identifies the saint as the founder, patroness, and abbess of the Benedictine order of nuns. The carved crozier, like the staff of Moses and Aaron (Exodus 4:17, 7:12), is a sign of higher power and a symbol of pastoral duties (J. Sauer) and belongs to the attributes of a bishop, as well as of an abbot and an abbess, who use it only within the walls of their cloisters.[7] An attribute of a more general nature is the large book the saint supports on her hip and upon which she fixes her gaze. This book symbolizes the Rules of the Order and identifies her as the founder. Unique in the known iconography of St. Scholastica is another attribute found only in our newly discovered figure, the globe at the base of the statue. The saint is shown looking in the opposite direction while disdainfully placing her foot on the globe lying at her feet, obviously signifying a complete renunciation of "all earthly goods, honors and pleasures."[8] We shall return to this presently.

The particular way the saint is represented evidently derives from the legend, modified by its popular eighteenth-century interpretation. We must assume that both the person commissioning the work and the artist had a detailed knowledge of the story, written in the quaint language of that period. The *Grosse Hauselegend,* a lexicon of saints, was extremely popular in southern Germany and neighboring Austria. It was written by Caspar Erhard, "the saintly doctor of letters and parson of Parr in Bavaria" (first edition: Augsburg, 1739).[9] In his account of St. Benedict and St. Scholastica (vol. 1, p. 145 ff.), they are described as brother and sister and as "two beautiful lights of the church and admirable examples of spiritual attainment." St. Scholastica is also referred to as having "a lively spirit and sweet appearance, with a happy disposition and righteous way of life." According to Erhard, even in her youth she preferred solitude to social life. This, he explains, was why she "renounced all jewels and rich garb," for "the exterior ornament of dress did not make one deserving of praise, but inner virtue and contemplation brought the greatest reward to a young maiden." Careful reading of such a contemporary interpretation of the saint's legend reveals the reason for the use of the globe in our sculpture. This seldom used attribute is actually a negative symbol, representing the world that St. Scholastica had renounced. Visually this is expressed by the way she steps on the sphere as though it were a toy ball, and thus a clear Scholastic meaning is maintained in this image of the Benedictine saint.

Before beginning a detailed comparison of the similarities the newly discovered figure shares with a number of other sculptures and preparatory drawings by Günther, we should mention a few sculptures of the same subject produced in the German-speaking lands of the eighteenth century. First to be cited are two figures of St. Scholastica,

*Recently purchased by the Los Angeles County Museum of Art with funds from the Times Mirror Foundation and Mrs. Camilla Chandler Frost.

2.

each with a St. Benedict as a counterpart, as is to be expected. These two pairs of quite dissimilar statues are by the Swabian sculptor Joseph Anton Feuchtmayr (1696-1770). This artist, often described as being the exact opposite of Günther, was court sculptor to the Elector of Bavaria at Munich. The statues just mentioned belong to the furnishings of Benedictine churches. One of the pairs, in Weingarten, is located above the dorsal of the south choir pews built in 1720,[10] and the other pair, begun in 1746, is in the nuns' gallery of the Benedictine cloister church in Fahr (Canton Aargau, Switzerland).[11] The expression and movement of Feuchtmayr's two figures of St. Scholastica hardly compare to the far superior works of the same subject made by Günther a bit later.

On the basis of the subject matter, we should also compare Günther's work with two stucco figures of about the same period by the Swabian sculptor Joseph Christian (1706-1777). His two holy abbesses — St. Scholastica and her counterpart, the seldom represented St. Gertrude of Helft — belong to the furnishings of the chapel of St. Benedict in what was once the Benedictine abbey church in Zweifalten. The faces of these two figures by Christian, as well as the face of St. Scholastica by Günther, have an unmistakable similarity to Bernini's famous St. Theresa in S. Maria della Vittoria in Rome, that embodiment of ecstasy whose extraordinary impact is due to "the almost literal translation of the nun's vision into plastic form," as E. Michalski has noted.[12] Bernini's representation of this face became an extremely important prototype for baroque sculpture, and it was known even by sculptors who never traveled to Rome, a fact that is indisputably demonstrated by J. J. Christian and Ignaz Günther.

The St. Scholastica by Günther was meant to be seen from below and at one time must have been placed at the gospel side of an apparently small altar, judging from the composition. Indeed, it stood against the wall and, as is customary in such cases, the back of the figure is not finished. The overall surface is carefully worked, clearly indicating that the figure was meant to be seen at close range. There was probably a pendant figure of St. Benedict of Nursia, the founder of the Benedictine order and St. Scholastica's twin brother. Based on this specific identification of the subject we are justified in supposing that such iconographically paired figures were once part of the furnishings of a Benedictine church with which Günther evidently had close ties. He was entrusted with the commission for the high altar with four figures (1755ff) for St. Andrew, the Benedictine high collegiate church in Freising, a work that was especially costly. In a letter preserved in the Ordinariatsarchiv in Munich (Act. Freising, St. Andrew) Günther states frankly that "As far as the price for the work is concerned, I hope to charge a satisfactorily reasonable rate since I must work well and cheaply in order to make myself known."[13] According to

3.

4.

1.
Ignaz Günther (1725-1775)
St. Scholastica, ca. 1775
Linden wood
h: 130 cm.; with crozier, 158 cm.
Los Angeles County Museum of Art
Purchased with funds from the Times Mirror Foundation and Mrs. Camilla Chandler Frost
M. 75. 103

2.
Ignaz Günther
Mary Immaculate, 1752-53
h: 191 cm.
Kopřivnà-Geppersdorf, Czechoslovakia,
Parish Church of the Most Holy Trinity

3.
Detail, right side of
St. Scholastica (fig. 1)

4.
Detail, left side of
Mary Immaculate (fig. 2)

5.

5.
Detail of garment drapery,
St. Scholastica (fig. 1)

6.
Ignaz Günther and A. Forster
God the Father with Scepter and Globe,
detail of a monstrance, ca. 1752-53
Kopřivnà-Geppersdorf, Czechoslovakia,
Parish Church of the Most Holy Trinity

7.
Ignaz Günther
Unidentified Saint (St. Andrew?), ca. 1755
h: 151 cm.
Munich-Nymphenburg, Chapel of the
Hospital of the Brothers of Charity

8.
Ignaz Günther
St. Peter with Inscription
(Matthew 16: 18), ca. 1755
h: 175 cm.
Munich-Nymphenburg, Chapel of the
Hospital of the Brothers of Charity

N. Backmund[14] the church's new decorations by J. B. Zimmermann and I. Günther, begun in 1756, must have been absolutely extraordinary. Besides the thirty-one devotional figures noted in a celebration speech in 1756, the church had no fewer than eleven altars. Contemporary accounts give no clue as to the subjects of the side altar sculptures, nor is there mention of the sculptors' names. The figures that once belonged to the newly decorated church cannot be traced, for this property was publicly auctioned during the secularization that took place between 25 February and 3 March 1803. Nonetheless it is quite possible that this newly discovered figure of St. Scholastica with her presumed pendant, a figure of St. Benedict of Nursia, once belonged to these church furnishings, now entirely dispersed. This conjecture is supported by iconographical reasons as well as by dating.

It is important to note, in fully appreciating Günther's oeuvre, the extraordinary degree to which it is defined by the use of types, not only in a formal sense but, although at first this seems surprising, in the conception and mode of representation of the subject matter as well. This consistent use of types thus becomes a criterion for identifying Günther's style. Theodor Hetzer[15] once wrote of G. B. Tiepolo that every variation in his work could be traced back to certain basic forms, and that his figures, however varied, still became "types, characteristic of certain generic forms." This is unequivocally true for Günther's work as well. It will soon become evident that the newly discovered St. Scholastica is critical to this discussion of Günther's consistent use of stock types throughout his career. It has already been noted that this figure undoubtedly belongs stylistically to his early period. In order to prove this, a comparison must be made with Günther's most important known piece of this time: the majestic figure of Mary Immaculate (fig. 2), over life-size (h. 191 cm.), from the high altar in the parish church of the Most Holy Trinity in Kopřivnà-Geppersdorf, Czechoslovakia. Unquestionably the two figures, although different in size, do resemble each other more closely than one would say at first glance. The slant of the head is similarly accentuated in both cases, while the extremely delicate gesture of the hands with their slightly spread fingers likewise indicates that both figures belong to the same sculptor's canon. This applies even more to the type of face and head found in both works, as the two profiles clearly show (figs. 3, 4). An almost identical formal vocabulary is applied to the projecting fold above the right leg in each figure. The concave folds are so deeply cut into the block that, if one so desired, a hand could be placed inside them; these typify Günther's characteristic use of extremely deep undercutting of garments (fig. 5). This is a "baroque" touch, contrasting with his treatment of drapery in his middle and late periods. During his early period the sculptor was still under the spell of his Munich

6.

7.

8.

9.

15.

9.
Ignaz Günther
Kneeling Madonna, detail from a preparatory sketch for a devotional picture of the "Augustinian Christ Child"
Munich, Staatliche Graphische Sammlung, inv. no. 5935

10.
Ignaz Günther
The "Saint of Starnberg" (detail), 1755
Starnberg, Wurmgaumuseum

11.
Detail, back of left side of *St. Scholastica* (fig. 1)

12.
Ignaz Günther
St. Anne, ca. 1758
Parish and Pilgrimage Church of St. Maria, Munich-Thalkirche

13.
Ignaz Günther
Mary as the Woman of the Apocalypse (detail), from the pulpit in Munich-Ramersdorf, 1760
Munich, private collection, Seidlein

14.
Ignaz Günther
St. Catherine of Siena (detail), 1760
Cloister Church of the Dominican nuns, Altenhohenau am Inn

15.
Detail, front of *St. Scholastica* (fig. 1)

10.

12.

14.

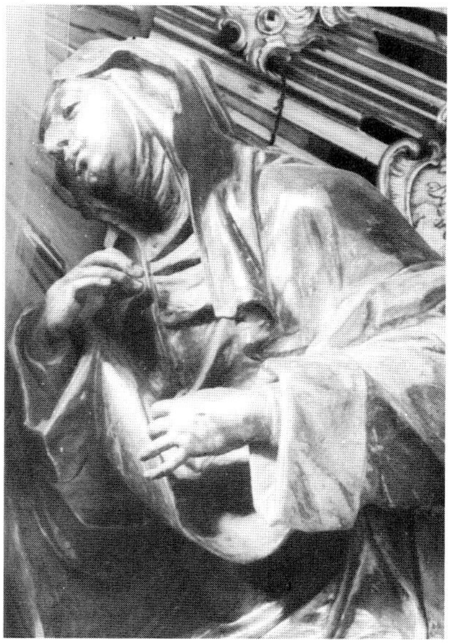

11.

13.

teacher Johann Baptist Straub, whose influence was widespread at the time. Examples of Günther's early drapery style, which serve as excellent comparisons, are not only the similarly draped folds of the God the Father figure on the embossed silver monstrance by Günther and Forster, ca. 1752-53 (fig. 6) in Kopřivnà-Geppersdorf, but also two figures of apostles that also date to the middle fifties. One is a kneeling figure (judging from the type it may be St. Andrew), 151 cm. high (fig. 7), and the other is a standing St. Peter, 175 cm. high (fig. 8). It is highly probable that they belong to the yet unpublished figures which once formed the furnishings, dispersed in 1809, of the cloister church of the Brothers of Charity of St. Max-vor-dem Sendlingertor in Munich. These figures, crowning examples of Günther's early oeuvre, were unknown until a few years ago. Recently restored, they are now in the chapel of the hospital of the Brothers of Charity in Munich-Nymphenburg.

There is an unmistakable affinity between the composition of the figure of St. Scholastica and a drawing by Günther (fig. 9), signed and dated 1755, in the Staatliche Graphische Sammlung, Munich (inv. no. 5935).[16] On this sheet, which is a sketch for a devotional picture, a kneeling Madonna is shown with both hands folded on her chest. She gazes at the "Augustinian Christ Child" lying at her feet; this was a miraculous [wax] image, much honored in Munich, which was once in the Augustinian Hermitage Convent Church. A comparison of the sculpture of St. Scholastica with the drawing truly offers a surprise, in that the two figures are so similar in type, expression, and the highly plastic treatment of their robes. The affinity of the two is such that the date 1755 that appears on the drawing provides a significant basis for dating the sculpture, which was obviously made at the same time.

We find ourselves in exactly the same year, 1755, in dating the so-called Saint of Starnberg (fig. 10) in the Starnberg Museum in Wurmgau, a sculpture that is rightly considered as one of Günther's major early works[17] and which can be compared with the St. Scholastica. It is not easy to explain the facial expression of the Starnberg Saint. It seems, as Zallinger-Thurn points out, that it is "veiled by an inexplicable sadness." The profile view of the head tilted to the right shows a drooping eyelid, a characteristically elongated nose without an indented bridge, and a sensitively depicted area around the mouth and chin. It is strikingly related by type to the face of St. Scholastica, as though the sculptor had twice used the same model (figs. 10, 11). An example of a further variation of this type used by Günther is a head of St. Anne, ca. 1758 (fig. 12), from the half-length figure on the high altar of the parish and pilgrimage church of St. Maria in Munich-Thalkirche, which offers us another definitive point of comparison.[18] The fact that in this representation the saint's dress approximates a nun's habit has not been previously mentioned. Günther also used this particular mode of dress in certain images of the Madonna which remain to be cited. A remarkable delineation of this stock type in Günther's work appears in his particularly characteristic head of a Woman of the Apocalypse, of 1760 (fig. 13), in a private collection in Munich; the figure was once in the parish and pilgrimage church in Munich-Ramersdorf. The "Berninesque" St. Catherine of Siena, also of 1760, from the high altar of the Dominican convent church in Altenhohenau am Inn,[19] is closely related in type (figs. 14, 15). Within this context we must also mention other figures, one, 18 cm. high (fig. 16), dating to the second half of the sixties, now in the Bavarian National Museum, which served as the model for a Mater Dolorosa for St. Jacob's chapel in Weyarn; another, similar in treatment and subject, in the parish church of St. Jacob in Vierkirchen near Dachau which is not reproduced here; and, lastly, the Sorrowful Mother (fig. 17) in St. Anton, Ingolstadt, which is signed and dated 1770.[20] If we compare the face of the St. Scholastica to Günther's nunlike figures of the Madonna, it becomes apparent that she could be a younger sister (fig. 18).

Following what has already been stated above, it is not inconsistent to introduce into the complex of stock types discussed here Günther's last work, the magnificent Pietà of the Friedhofskapelle in Nenningen (1774). This work was carried out in three stages: first the preparatory drawing (fig. 19) in the Staatliche Graphische Sammlung in Munich (inv. no. 32.213);[21] then the model carved in linden wood (fig. 20) which was acquired by the Bayerisches Nationalmuseum, Munich, in 1974; and finally the finished version (fig. 21). The artistic process clearly illustrated here parallels the actual stages of variation of a stock type. Thus it is not surprising that even the faces of St. Scholastica (fig. 22) and of the Madonna represented as a nun in the Nenningen Pietà are very similar even though so many years separate the time of their execution.

The last work in the series of Günther's large altars is the high altar (1768-70) in the former church of the Benedictine abbey in Mallersdorf. Adolf Feulner[22] has already correctly noted that it is not a work of "the early but of the final period." This judgment is entirely acceptable, and particularly applies to the sculptural decoration consisting of four over-life-size white polished figures, grouped in pairs. The figures on either side of the altarpiece reinforce our observation that in the furnishing of Benedictine churches, St. Benedict of Nursia was most often a pendant of St. Scholastica, who ranks as the second of these two major figures in Western monasticism. Because of the strongly pronounced turn of the head, the direction of the gaze, and the rhetorical gesture of the raised right arm which originally held the staff, we relate

16.

18.

17.

16.
Ignaz Günther
Mater Dolorosa, model for the figure of the same subject in St. Jacob's Chapel, Weyarn
h: 18 cm.
Bayerisches Nationalmuseum

17.
Ignaz Günther
Mater Dolorosa, signed and dated 1770
Parish Church of St. Anton, Ingolstadt

18.
Detail, *St. Scholastica* (fig. 1)

19.

20.

the Mallersdorf St. Scholastica (fig. 23) to the larger composition, belonging to the central part of the altar. General attributes are the abbess' staff, the golden cross hanging on a ribbon from her neck, and the Book of Rules in her left hand. The dove with open wings sitting on the book is, however, a singular accessory recalling the vision that appeared to St. Benedict at the moment of his sister's death. According to Dialogue II in St. Gregory's account, St. Benedict, in his cell, saw his sister's departing soul in the form of a dove flying to Heaven. Until now, the St. Scholastica of Mallersdorf was the only known representation of this saint by Ignaz Günther. Thus it is important to compare the Mallersdorf figure with the other sculptures of similar subject matter which we have discussed. The Mallersdorf figure shows an obvious stylistic change that is characteristic of Günther's late period. The treatment of the garment is limited here to great masses of cloth which are not at all as deeply undercut as the earlier ones. At the same time the forms of the body seem to be much more strongly expressed, the movement of the leg is quite noticeable, with its upper and lower parts clearly outlined under the robe. In contrast to the rich and nervous movement that appears in the contours of the early St. Scholastica, the composition of the later work has a much quieter character. This is also expressed in the flowing compactness of the silhouette. In summary, Günther's late figure, meant to be seen from a single viewpoint, appears to be much flatter than the works executed fifteen years earlier.

Apart from these stylistic observations, we also find a surprising motif in the Mallersdorf nun. This new element can be traced to a small devotional picture (14 x 9 cm.) which obviously served as the prototype, although it has not been previously recognized as such. The print (fig. 24), dating to the mid-eighteenth century, is signed "Klauber Cath. [olici]," an identification used in Augsburg by the brothers Joseph Sebastian Klauber (ca. 1700-1768) and Johann Baptist Klauber (1712-after 1787). The fact that Günther did not slavishly follow the model presumably prescribed by the donor, but instead modified it, can be seen, for example, in the way he reversed the contraposto.

As far as the representation of the subject is concerned, Günther's early and late figures of Scholastica are at opposing poles. In the early St. Scholastica, the subject matter, composition, and technique are forcefully brought together in a most admirable way. Thus it ranks among the best Günther has created in the realm of religious sculpture. The Mallersdorf figure depends too much on the model taken from the Augsburg devotional picture and, compared to the early St. Scholastica, its quality suffers considerably. It is as if the power of artistic imagination were already quite spent.

19.
Ignaz Günther
Sketch for the
Pietà in Nenningen, ca. 1774
Pen and ink wash
Munich, Staatliche Graphische
Sammlung, inv. no. 32.213

20.
Ignaz Günther
Model for the *Pietà* in Nenningen, 1774
Linden wood
h: 25.5 cm.
Bayerisches Nationalmuseum, Munich,
new acquisition, 1974

21.
Ignaz Günther
Pietà, detail of the Madonna's head in
profile
Friedhofskapelle, Nenningen (cemetery
chapel)

21.

22.

23.

24.

25.

26.

27.

22.
St. Scholastica (fig. 1)

23.
Ignaz Günther
St. Scholastica, 1768-70
Former Benedictine abbey church, Mallersdorf

24.
Klauber
St. Scholastica, Augsburg, mid-18th century
Print, 14 x 9 cm.

25.
Head of St. Scholastica's crozier (fig. 1), front view

26.
Head of St. Scholastica's crozier (fig. 23), back view

27.
Head of St. Scholastica's crozier (fig. 1), back view

28.

Before concluding our observations we must point out a certain formal characteristic in Günther's works. The carved staff heads, each with an open, flattened flower, are the crowning elements of the abbesses' croziers in both the early and late figures of Scholastica; they are remarkably alike in form. The repeated use of almost identical carved crozier heads in other figures by Günther (figs. 25-27) is a most important fact which needs further investigation. This motif appears on croziers held by St. Korbinian (1759ff.) on the high altar in Rott am Inn and by the St. Benedict of Nursia in Mallersdorf and serves as an identifying sign of rank. The special position held by a workshop like the one headed by Günther in Munich is due to the maintenance of an even level of quality and harmony of form in each and every object turned out, down to the mere accessories of a large figure.

In order to complete the still unfinished discussion of the iconography of St. Scholastica,[23] a comparison must be made between Ignaz Günther's late representation of this subject, in Mallersdorf, and its predecessor, which is certainly a welcome addition to the repertory of his known works (figs. 28, 29). Considered from the point of view of iconography, the brilliant earlier work must be recognized as displaying the artist's ability to represent Scholastica in a most convincing manner. Therefore we do not consider it an exaggeration to declare that the St. Scholastica dated ca. 1755 belongs to the most fortunate of discoveries. We know of nothing even slightly comparable produced at the time. One has the impression that to this work, which has again become part of his known oeuvre, Ignaz Günther truly wanted to give his best.

This article was published in its original German as "Eine unbekannte hl. Scholastika aus der Frühzeit Günthers" in *Alte und Moderne Kunst,* vol. 136/137 (1974), 303-13. The English translation by Alla Theodora Hall and Esther deVecsey is printed here with the generous permission of the author and the publisher.
Dr. Woeckel, research scholar at the Zentralinstitut für Kunstgeschichte in Munich, has devoted the larger part of his life to the study of German Baroque sculpture, especially that of Ignaz Günther. His most recent of a long series of publications on that master is a definitive study of his drawings and their relation to his sculptures, *Ignaz Günther, Die Handzeichnungen des kurfürsteich bayerischen Hofbildhauers Franz Ignaz Günther (1725-1775),* Weisenhorn, 1975.

29.

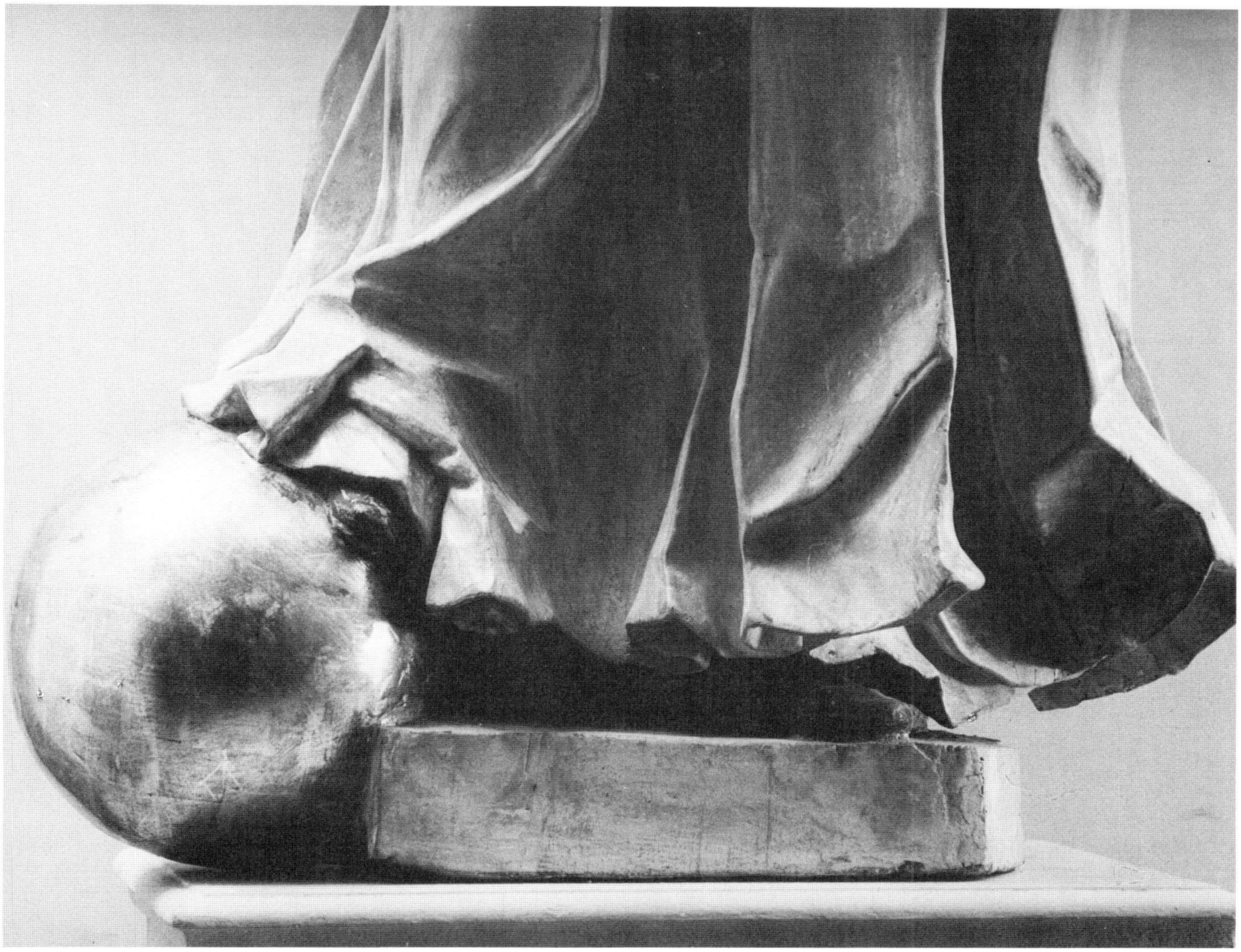

28.
Detail, back of St. Scholastica (fig. 1)

29.
Detail of base, drapery,
and globe, St. Scholastica (fig. 1)

Notes

1.
G. P. Woeckel and H. Herzog, "Ignaz Günthers Frühwerk in Kopřivna (Geppersdorf)/CSSR (I and II)," *Pantheon,* XXIV, 1966, 217-52, 303-13.

2.
K. Sitzman, "Unbekannte Werke von Ignaz Günther in Rotlenbach," *Frankische Blätter,* III, 1951, n. 20, 83-84.

3.
H. Decker, "Ein unbekanntes Frühwerk Ignaz Günthers," *Die Kunst und das Schöne Heim,* LV, 1955, 332-33.

4.
G. P. Woeckel, "Neue Funde zum Werk Ignaz Günthers," *Das Münster,* VII, 1954, 69-79; idem, "Christusdarstellungen v. Ignaz Günther," *Das Münster,* XX, 1967, 369-88.

5.
The saint was born about 480 and died shortly before St. Benedict, around 543. She dedicated herself to God as a child, according to St. Gregory the Great, Dialogue II, 33. She transferred from her earlier cloister at Subiaco (Roccabotte) to Montecassino and, like St. Benedict, was buried there. The Longobards destroyed that abbey in 580, and around 730 the relics of the saintly pair were transferred to Fleury-sur-Loire (afterwards Saint-Benoit-sur-Loire) by Frankonian monks. The majority of St. Scholastica's relics arrived at Juvigny-sur-Loison in the year 874, and a smaller portion were taken to Le Mans in 1906. See *Lexikon für Theologie und Kirche,* IX, 1937, sp. 305 and *Bibliotheca Sanctorum,* XI, Rome, 1968, 1/742-49. Connected with the saint's legend is the fact that she is known as the patroness of rain and protectress against lightning.

6.
J. Braun, *Tracht und Attribute der Heiligen in der deutschen Kunst,* Stuttgart, 1943, 796.

7.
F. von Sales Doye, *Die alten Trachten der männlichen und weiblichen Orden sowie der geistlichen Mitglieder der ritterlichen Orden,* Leipzig, 1930, 53, fig. 256, pl. 128.

8.
Braun, *Tracht und Attribute,* 827. Here the same attribute is mentioned regarding St. Bruno.

9.
In the same series: J. Giulini, *Tagliche Erbauung eines wahren Christen,* Augsburg, 1753; 2nd ed., Augsburg, 1762-64. See I, 135-36 (February 10 is the feast day of St. Scholastica). Illustrated by a print (17.5 x 10.5 cm.) by Johann Jacob Ebersbach (1717-1754), after the original design by Johann Wolfgang Baumgartner (1712-1761). The print shows the last meeting of the brother and sister, which is described by Gregory the Great in his Dialogues. Another scene from the life of St. Benedict is depicted in a painting dating after 1700 by Lazzaro Baldi (ca. 1624-1723) in the chapel of St. Benedict in S. Maria di Campo Marzo in Rome. St. Scholastica, dressed in the complete habit of her order, appears to her brother, St. Benedict, who is praying before an altar at the hour of his death. She bestows her blessing on the dying man who has his arms outstretched in prayer. The sketch for this painting was formerly in a private collection in Berlin. See H. Voss, *Die Malerei des Barock in Rom,* Berlin, 1924, 557, with fig. on 277. Another depiction, idyllic and happy, of the siblings dates to sometime later and was painted by Josef Ignaz Mildorfer (1719-1775) as an altarpiece in 1755. It is located in the left chapel by the belfry, in the parish and pilgrimage church of Our Blessed Lady in Hafnerberg (a district of Altenmarkt an der Triesting/ Nieder Osterreich). See E. Eccel, "Josef Ignaz Mildorfer und das Hochaltarblatt von Neustift bei Brixen," *Cultura Altesina, XVII,* 1963, 21-48, especially p. 36 with fig. 5, table XI. — *OKT* XVIII (Baden in NO), Vienna, 1924, 298.

10.
W. Boeck, *Joseph Anton Feuchtmayer,* Tübingen, 48, with ill. 27, 28, and 38.

11.
Idem, *Feuchtmayr-Meisterwerke,* Tubingen, 24-25, with ill. 49.

12.
E. Michalski, *Joseph Christian,* Leipzig, 1926, 58, with ill. 102-03; G. P. Woeckel, *Johann Joseph Christian von Riedlingen —Ein Oberschwäbischer Bildhauer des Rokoko,* Lindau and Konstanz, 1958, 104, with ill. 32, 33, 35.

13.
S. Schönberger, *Ignaz Günther,* Munich, 1954, 25-27. The high altar was to have had four figures, over life-size, representing SS. Lawrence, Sixtus, Corbinian, and Batho grouped around the Trinity. Following secularization, the altar of the Congregational church was acquired for 75 (!) gulden by the local parish church. There, Günther's altar burned in 1865.

14.
N. Backmund, *Die Kollegiat — und Kanonissenstifte in Bayern,* Windberg, 1973, 57-59; J. B. Prechtl, *Das Kanonikatsstift St. Andrea auf dem Domberge in Freising,* Freising, 1888, 101.

15.
T. Hetzer, *Die Fresken Tiepolos in der Würzburger Residenz,* Frankfurt, 1943, 39.

16.
G. P. Woeckel, *Die Handzeichnungen des kurbayerischen Hofbildhauers Franz Ignaz Günther,* (Bayern, Germany: Anton H. Konrad Verlag, 1975), cat. no. 79.

17.
Schönberger, *Ignaz Günther,* 24, figs. 6 and 7.

18.
Schönberger, *Ignaz Günther,* 21-31, 138-39. This dating cannot be proved on stylistic grounds.

19.
Ibid., 35-36, with ill. 19, and 65 ff. with ill. 96 and 97.

20.
Ibid., 51, with figs. 72 and 73, 73-74, with figs. 102 and 103; Woeckel, *Das Münster,* 1954, 72 ff.; J. Blatner, "Beiträge zum Werk von Ignaz Günther," *Deutsche Kunst und Denkmalpflege,* I, 1956, 59-61, wherein the formerly thought provenance in the St. Nikolas Church in Spalt is disproven, but we will not dwell on this here.

21.
Woeckel, *Die Handzeichnungen,* cat. no. 29.

22.
A. Feulner, *Ignaz Günther (II),* Munich, 1947, 87; Schönberger, *Ignaz Günther,* 71-73, with figs. 126-29.

23.
Noteworthy, though without German examples, is B. Heurtebize and R. Triger, *Sainte Scholastique, Partonne (sic) du Mans. Sa vie-son culte, Son rôle dans l'histoire de la cité. Solesmes,* 1891, 2nd edition, Le Mans, 1923.

A Buddhist Thai Altarpiece and Five Related Bronzes

Virginia Dofflemyer
Curatorial Assistant, Indian and Islamic Art

The primary intent of this brief article is to introduce a Buddhist altarpiece (figs. 1 and 2) from the Lop'buri region of present day central Thailand, recently donated by Christian Humann. This elaborate shrine, once housed in the famous Thompson Collection in Bangkok, is the first major Southeast Asian bronze to be acquired by the Museum. Apart from augmenting the Museum's rather modest holdings in Southeast Asian art, this particular shrine also raises several intriguing art historical questions.

The Los Angeles shrine is an impressive example of the technical proficiency of the Lop'buri craftsman, despite slight damage to the reverse of its multi-tiered pedestal. Originally this bronze was inlaid with either precious or semi-precious stones, as is evidenced by the two conspicuously empty rosette-framed settings at the apex of the shrine. The entire sculpture has acquired over the years a richly variegated patina which is enhanced by slight traces of what must have once been a brilliant gilt finish. The complicated design of the altarpiece gives testimony to the Lop'buri artists' mastery of the *cire perdu* casting technique, the ensemble being comprised of four individually cast parts: The Buddha Śākyamuni and his lotus seat; the large ogival *écran* which provides an architectural setting for this seated figure; the small but flamboyant reptilian arcature that rises from the raised pilaster capitals; and the multi-tiered pedestal into which the elaborate *écran* and Buddha figure are fitted.[1]

The Buddha Śākyamuni, seated firm and erect like a model yogi, wears the *saṅghāṭi* in the open mode. His right hand displays the earth-touching gesture *(bhūmisparśa-mudrā),* while his left rests on his lap, palm upwards. The earth-touching gesture is emblematic of his conquest over Māra, the Buddhist god of desire who tried to tempt Śākyamuni during his enlightenment under the Bodhi tree at Bodhgaya. According to Buddhist legend, by touching the earth with his right hand the Buddha called upon the earth to witness his resistance of Māra's temptations, for the only other available witnesses were Māra's own followers. From behind this Buddha image rises an elaborate aureole, its outline enhanced by an intricately incised flame border. Curious are both the lobes of the raised ridge from which these flames proceed and the symmetrical arrangement of the five circular forms incised beneath those lobes (fig. 2).[2]

Concealed by the Buddha's head and visible only when the bronze is disassembled is the conventional nimbus that indicates the figure's divinity. Above the Buddha's head and slightly overlying the apex of this nimbus is an ornate *makara* arcature which slips into the raised pilasters that frame the centrally placed Buddha figure. Although this popular reptilian motif is here given a slightly avian character, the two *makaras* that appear at the base of the flame aureole are somewhat more conventional. Supporting both the aureole and the seated Buddha figure is a geometrically incised and multi-tiered pedestal. Not only has the contour of this elaborate throne been given visual interest by the stepped arrangement of its several horizontal registers, but it has been further enhanced by the subtle recession of its several longitudinal planes.

The Los Angeles Buddha figure has slightly elongated proportions, a small waist, and attenuated limbs. While the face itself is full, the jawline is somewhat squared. The nose is broad, the browline straight, while the mouth curves upwards in a faint smile. The individual spiral curls of the Buddha's coiffure have been arranged in a geometrical design, the whole crowned by a rather unusual *uṣṇīṣa* or cranial bump, one of the eight major marks denoting the Buddha's superhuman nature. Although usually semi-circular and adorned with separate curls, the *uṣṇīṣa* in this instance is shaped like an inverted cone, its surface marked only by three horizontal bands.

When this altarpiece was first published several years ago, it was given the following attribution: "Late Khmer Lopburi period. From North Eastern Thailand."[3] According to the dating system supplied in the preface of the catalog in which it appears, the "Khmer Lopburi period" has been assigned a tenth- to fourteenth-century date. The attribution, "late Khmer Lopburi period," therefore seems to indicate that a thirteenth- to fourteenth-century date was intended for this shrine. Although sculpture produced by a tradition as stringently religious as the Mon-Khmer center of Lop'buri can never be dated with absolute certainty, we will see that a thirteenth-century date is, in fact, very reasonable for this altarpiece. The rather unusual phrase, "Khmer Lopburi period," suggests that the bronze was believed to exemplify the Lop'buri style and that it may have been produced while that area was under the cultural influence of the Khmers of Cambodia. Despite the fact that this bronze was found in northeastern Thailand, both its structural and decorative elements seem to confirm the Lop'buri attribution. But in order to better understand such an attribution, it will be useful at this point to introduce two other Lop'buri-style shrines into our discussion of the Museum's new altarpiece, and subsequently to place all three within their historical context.

The two additional Lop'buri shrines to be discussed are presently part of the Pan-Asian Collection. Like the Los Angeles altarpiece both were cast in several sections. The double-sided shrine (figs. 3, 4) consists of three separate parts, the other (fig. 5) of four. Similarly, both bronzes were originally inlaid with precious or semi-precious stones and may have been gilded. Beyond such technical features, a cursory glance at this group of Lop'buri shrines reveals certain other basic similarities: a central, seated Buddha; a flame-bordered aureole; and a multi-tiered and recessed pedestal. It will become increasingly apparent as we discuss these Lop'buri examples that, apart from these

1.

1.
Buddhist Altarpiece
Thailand, Lop'buri style, 13th century
Bronze
h: 19⅛ in. (48.6 cm.)
Gift of Christian Humann
Los Angeles County Museum of Art

2.
Detail of fig.1

obvious similarities, there is great stylistic variety. This eclecticism will be made clearer after we review the history of the Lop'buri region.

Between the sixth and tenth centuries the area that is now central Thailand was both politically and culturally dominated by the Mon people of the Dvāravatī kingdom. Theirs was an artistic tradition largely inspired by that of Gupta India. As is evidenced by the numerous Buddhist artifacts from this region, the Buddha cult was apparently quite pervasive. These Dvāravatī sculptures, whether of stone or of bronze, generally depict the Buddha standing, with both hands raised in the same gesture. Some representations of seated Buddhas display *dhyānamudrā,* the gesture of meditation, while others exhibit *vitarkamudrā,* the gesture of explication. Depictions of the Māradharṣaṇa scene, or the temptation of Māra, are relatively few. In fact, prior to the eleventh century, when this Mon empire was already on the wane, that particular incident from the life of Śākyamuni appears to have been virtually unknown to Dvāravatī craftsmen.

With the eleventh-century dissolution of the Mon Dvāravatī empire at this time, a new Mon settlement, Luovo, developed in the northern reaches of the Dvāravatī empire, centered in the ancient site of Lop'buri. However, the political independence of this new settlement was short-lived, surviving the successive waves of Khmer aggression for less than a hundred years. Luovo fell prey to Khmer aggrandizement during the reign of Sūryavarman I (1011-1050), consequently becoming a major outpost of the ever-expanding Khmer empire and so remaining for almost two hundred years. Sūryavarman I was not only the first Buddhist king of ancient Kāmbujadeśa (modern Cambodia), but he was also a Mahāyānist and a foreigner who, in an attempt to conciliate his subjects, prudently practiced religious tolerance.[4] Thus, despite the Mahāyānist inclinations of the Khmer king, the Mon population of Luovo, deeply entrenched in their ancestral traditions, remained predominantly Hīnayāna Buddhist.

Even before the time of Sūryavarman I various Thai tribes from the north had been filtering into central Thailand where they established numerous small city-states. After the reign of Jayavarman VII (1181-1215), when the Khmer empire began to lose its stronghold on its outlying regions, certain of these tribes began to assert themselves. Around the middle of the thirteenth century a Thai chieftain from one of these tribes established the capital of the first unified Thai kingdom, known as Siam (ca. 1220-1350),[5] at Sukodhai in northern Thailand. Although the Sukodhai kingdom was quite short-lived, its conquests were many. Like the regions to the north and south, Luovo fell under the political domination of this empire. But by 1349 the last of the Sukodhai kings had been forced to acknowledge the suzerainity of a new state that had sprung up in the lower reaches of its empire. Thus the second Thai

2.

3.

4.

kingdom of Ayudhyā (14th-17th century) was established, with Ayudhyā as its capital. The Mon — Khmer civilization of Luovo was subsequently absorbed into the new territories of this empire, but Lop'buri, which had formed an integral part of both the Dvāravatī and Sukodhai kingdoms, continued to retain its cultural importance. as is evident from the artistic activity that continued to flourish there. Apart from Lop'buri, several other cultural centers thrived under the patronage of the Ayudhya empire. Of these, two had anterior traditions contemporaneous with that of Lop'buri: U'Tong (11th-14th century) and Chiangsan (10th-17th century). In addition to these, a third center developed at the capital, Ayudhyā (14th-17th century).

When Lop'buri came under the political and cultural domination of the Khmers in the eleventh century, this area was still greatly influenced by its Mon Dvāravatī heritage. While Lop'buri could never totally disregard this earlier tradition, the eleventh- to fourteenth-century products of this region testify to the tremendous impact of the Khmer empire on the art of Lop'buri. Although Lop'buri artists found inspiration primarily in these artistic traditions, other contemporary artistic centers within Thailand, like U'Tong and Chiangsan, must also have somewhat influenced the style of Lop'buri. And finally, one cannot completely ignore the existence of two major Buddhist civilizations that were flourishing at this time, namely, the Burmese kingdom to the north, centered in Pagán, and the Śailendra empire of Śrīvijaya to the south. The artistic traditions that developed in these regions must have similarly provided the Lop'buri artist with additional material.

In order to better understand the extent to which the Khmer artistic tradition was fused into the products of the Lop'buri school, and to determine the salient features that characterize the Lop'buri style, it will be useful to discuss briefly three Khmer bronzes of a similar iconographical type and from approximately the same period as the Los Angeles shrine. Two of these are housed in the Cleveland Museum of Art (figs. 6, 7), the third in the Kimbell Art Foundation (fig. 8).[6] While two of the three are actually altarpieces (figs. 7, 8), not unlike the Los Angeles bronze, the third (fig. 6) is a finial that may once have decorated a palanquin. Of the three Buddhist representations only one depicts the Buddha figure as an ascetic (fig. 6), devoid of regal accoutrements; the other two (figs. 7, 8) portray a crowned Buddha with all the regalia of royalty. The Buddhas depicted in both the Cleveland finial (fig. 6) and the Kimbell shrine (fig. 8) display *bhūmisparśamudrā* with their right hands, emblematic of the temptation or Māradharṣaṇa incident; the Buddha in the Cleveland altarpiece (fig. 7), however, is represented in *dhyānamudrā,* symbolic of the Buddha's actual enlightenment. Thus, two of these Khmer images do exhibit the same Māradharṣaṇa

5.

6.

scene evinced in the Los Angeles shrine. Artists of both Khmer bronzes have placed additional emphasis on the temptation scene by incorporating into their designs the followers of Māra below each of the seated Buddha figures. All three Khmer bronzes include the tree motif, thus serving a didactic purpose by assigning the incident to the Buddha's seven-week fast. Each week of that fast Śākyamuni allegedly seated himself beneath a different tree and a different incident occurred. While the temptation of Māra is generally attributed to the fourth or fifth week of this fast, the enlightenment is always relegated to the last. The incorporation of a tree into the iconography of these bronzes served a didactic purpose by placing the incident within the context of this seven-week fast.

Technically, each of these bronzes testifies to the Khmer artist's proficiency in bronze casting. The Kimbell shrine, for instance, not only has eighteen separate parts, but also stands over five feet tall and was originally inset with precious or semi-precious stones.

Noteworthy is the fact that both of these Khmer shrines (figs. 7, 8) simulate the façade of a Khmer *prasat* or tower. The post and lintel arrangement of pillar or pilaster elements supporting cantilevered reptilian *toraṇa* when used in conjunction with the geometrical design of the bases is reminiscent of the entrances to such towers.

Beyond such technical and structural elements, we cannot help noting the Khmer fascination with decorative elements. While we have already mentioned the iconographical need for incorporating the tree motif into Māradharṣaṇa scenes, their inclusion serves another, purely decorative function. Like the tree motif, the mythical reptile, the *makara*, provided the Khmer artist with an excuse for embellishment, as is evidenced in each of these two shrines. The polycephalous *nāga*, or cobra, which appears in the Cleveland finial (fig. 6), is yet another popular decorative device. And while it is not immediately detected in every instance, each of these Khmer examples incorporates a flame or flame-shaped leaf motif in its sculptural program.

We have previously noted that the Māradharṣaṇa theme was rarely depicted by the Mon Dvāravatī artist. It is of interest to note that the appearance of this iconographical type in the traditions of both Kāmbujadeśa and Lop'buri may reflect the simultaneous influence of an outside source. But curiously, it seems to have been far more popular at Lop'buri than in the Khmer empire. Of further interest is the fact that this iconographical type occurs among the artistic products of U'Tong and Chiangsan and continued to enjoy popular acclaim in Thailand. While the general treatment of the Māradharṣaṇa theme by both Lop'buri and Khmer artists is essentially quite similar, there are some basic differences. More often than not the Khmer artist elected to represent the Buddha as both crowned and regally attired, while Lop'buri versions of this legend gen-

3.
Buddhist Altarpiece (front)
Thailand, Lop'buri style,
11th-13th century
Bronze
h: 15⅛ in. (38.4 cm.)
Pan-Asian Collection

4.
Reverse of fig. 3

5.
Buddhist Altarpiece
Thailand, Lop'buri style,
13th-14th century
Bronze
h: 21⅛ in. (53.7 cm.)
Pan-Asian Collection

6.
Finial
Khmer, style of Angkor Thom, Bayon,
late 12th-early 13th century
Bronze
h: 15 7/16 in. (39.2 cm.)
Cleveland Museum of Art
Purchase, Andrew R. and Martha Holden
Jennings Fund

7.
Buddhist Altarpiece
Khmer, style of Angkor Wat,
first half of the 12th century
Bronze
h: 10½ in. (26.7 cm.)
Cleveland Museum of Art
Purchase from the S. H. Wade Fund

7.

erally portray the Buddha as an ascetic.[8] Also of interest is the curious desire of the Khmer artist to place the Buddha within an explicit narrative context by incorporating the followers of Māra into such representations. The Lop'buri artist, on the other hand, seems to have had no such desire and omits these figures altogether.

Such iconographic dissimilarities may reflect completely different sources or perhaps only different interpretations of the same source. Certainly one must wonder at the prevalence of the Māradharṣaṇa theme among extant sculptures recovered from the "Khmerized" site of Lop'buri. Whether this has anything to do with the doctrinaire difference between the Māhayānism under Sūryavarman I in Cambodia proper and the Hīnayāna Buddhism that prevailed in the Lop'buri region is impossible to determine. After all, there is no reason why the Māradharṣaṇa scene should not have been equally popular with all sects of Buddhism. Interestingly, the prevalence of this Buddhist legend in the Hīnayāna artistic tradition of Burma is clearly the result of direct contact with the northeast Indian Pāla tradition. A popular theme in eighth- and ninth-century Pāla India, the Māradharṣaṇa type seems to have been subsequently imported by Burmese monks who are known to have visited various of the monastic Buddhist centers of northeast India. But whether the seemingly simultaneous appearance of this iconographic type in both the "Khmerized" region of Lop'buri and Cambodia proper can be attributed to influences from either Burma or Pāla India is difficult to say. In fact, it might be explained by one or more of several alternate hypotheses. On the one hand, the Māradharṣaṇa type may have traveled from Pāla India to these regions via Burma; on the other, it may have been imported directly from India itself. Or still again, it may have been introduced into these Southeast Asian areas from both regions.

Similarly, the concept of the crowned and regal Buddha, which is almost consistently reflected in Khmer representations of the Māradharṣaṇa theme and to a lesser extent in Lop'buri ones, may be traced to Pāla or Burmese sources. As is evidenced by a tenth-century relief from Bihar in East India in the Museum's collection (fig. 9) the Pāla-style Buddha of the Māradharṣaṇa incident is often crowned and placed within an architectural setting. Since the Pāla invention of crowning the Buddha was contemporaneous with the increased popularity accorded the Māradharṣaṇa theme, it is understandable that Burmese monks should have similarly appropriated this manner of Buddha depiction.[9] It is probable, therefore, that the idea of the crowned and regal Buddha, like the Māradharṣaṇa theme itself, was introduced into both Lop'buri and Cambodia in a similar fashion.

Unlike the Māradharṣaṇa theme and the concept of the crowned Buddha, which can both be ascribed to either Burmese and/or Pāla Indian influences, the Lop'buri fascination with the multi-part bronze casting technique may be Khmer in inspiration. The Lop'buri predilection for decoration, however, clearly reflects Khmer preoccupation with the same. Certainly this proclivity for the ornate was not one that Lop'buri could have inherited from its Dvāravatī ancestors. As we compare certain of the previously discussed Khmer and Lop'buri bronzes we shall see that immigrant Khmers obviously exerted considerable influence upon the artistic tradition of eleventh- to fourteenth-century Lop'buri. Although *makara, nāga,* and pilaster motifs; the *prasat* shape of the shrine; and the tiered and recessed pedestal are all features that appeared earlier in the Khmer sculptural tradition than in that of Lop'buri, we must remember that such structural and decorative features do occur in slightly modified forms in the contemporaneous artistic tradition of Pāla India.[10] Because of the similar arrangement of these Khmer and Lop'buri elements, however, it seems likely that the thirteenth- to fourteenth-century Lop'buri shrines here under discussion were likely inspired by contemporaneous and earlier Khmer examples, not unlike those we have previously cited.

At the same time, it must also be pointed out that there is a fundamental difference between the Khmer and Lop'buri attitudes toward the Buddha figure itself. While typical Khmer figures are usually rather squat and robust, displaying somewhat squared features, Lop'buri ones have slightly more elongated proportions. But obviously the classically proportioned and sensuously modeled images of their Mon Dvāravatī predecessors were familiar to these Lop'buri artists. And it is not surprising that this ancient Dvāravatī attitude toward the Buddha figure continued to influence Lop'buri taste between the eleventh and fourteenth centuries. Thus, it is not surprising that the elongated proportions of contemporaneous U'Tong and Chiangsan figures should have held greater appeal for the Lop'buri artist than did the more robust images produced under Khmer patronage. While this preference for classically modeled and elegantly proportioned figures is quite apparent in the Museum's Lop'buri bronze (fig. 1), it is even more pronounced in the single-sided Pan-Asian shrine (fig. 5). On the other hand, the crowned Buddha figure of the double-sided altarpiece (fig. 3) displays a greater affinity with the Khmer figure type (compare figs. 1-8).

Thus, despite the continued presence of the Khmers in the Lop'buri region and the tremendous impact they exerted on the Lop'buri sculptural tradition, the Lop'buri artists themselves remained vitally creative. A brief comparison of the Lop'buri altarpieces included here should make this fact immediately evident. For instance, the idea of decorating both sides of a votive shrine (figs. 3, 4) seems to be totally original with the Lop'buri artist. Certainly this feature is not found among the sculptures pro-

8.
Buddhist Altarpiece
Khmer, Post-Bayon style,
13th-14th century
Bronze
h: 68½ in. (174 cm.)
Kimbell Art Foundation,
Fort Worth, Texas

8.

9.

duced by the Mon Dvāravatī empire, nor in the contemporaneous sculptural tradition of Kāmbujadeśa, nor among the products of the Indian peninsula. Interestingly, this feature does continue to appear intermittently in the later art of Thailand.[8] One must, however, wonder why the Lop'buri artist chose to decorate the reverse of such a bronze if it was not intended to be seen. And if it was meant to be viewed in a temple atmosphere, how was it situated?

Further evidence of the Lop'buri artist's ingenuity and inventiveness is quite easily detected and does not need to be dealt with here in any great detail. Quite simply, it should be noted that all three Buddha figures (figs. 1, 3, 5) exhibit a slightly different canon of proportions. While all three shrines display multi-tiered and recessed pedestals, each is clearly distinct from the other. Similarly, while each Buddha figure has been provided with an ornate lotus seat, their designs have little in common with one another. All three altarpieces do, however, employ many of the same decorative motifs evidenced in the previously discussed Khmer examples: the flame-bordered aureole; the tree; the *makara;* the *nāga;* the framing pilaster device. But the treatment and combinations of each of these elements is remarkably different, for in borrowing these various Khmer features, the Lop'buri artist has managed to rearrange and reinterpret them with a new vitality and spontaneity.

By way of conclusion, it would seem relevant to view the Museum's newly acquired altarpiece within the context of Lop'buri stylistic development, and to assign it at least a general date. From the preceding discussion it should be apparent that the sculptural tradition of the Thai school of Lop'buri is characterized by eclecticism. Because of this and the fact that there are no known dated Lop'buri-style sculptures and very few known inscriptions, assigning exact dates to such Lop'buri shrines is virtually impossible. At best we can hope to establish relative dates based upon available historical data and stylistic comparison.

Each of the Lop'buri shrines we have examined exhibits various combinations of influences from Pāla India and/or Burma, Cambodia proper, and the Thai schools of U'Tong and Chiangsan. While we have already observed that both the basic iconography and certain structural features were likely imported from either northeast India or Burma, the proportions and modeling are a curious mixture of Mon, Khmer, and Thai elements. The decorative motifs, on the other hand, while probably Indian in origin, are for the most part Khmer in inspiration and Lop'buri in interpretation.

Whether it was known as Dvāravatī or Luovo, the Lop'buri region was basically a Mon settlement prior to the Khmer conquest (ca. 1097). It would therefore seem reasonable to assign a tenth- to eleventh-century date to any object exhibiting primarily Mon features. A piece displaying predominantly Khmer features, on the other hand, would likely be contemporaneous with the Khmer hegemony in this region (ca. 1097-1220). An image exhibiting marked influences from certain of the other Thai schools, however, should probably be assigned a date corresponding to the establishment of the Sukodhai and Ayudhyā kingdoms (ca. 1220-1349; 1349-17th century), when contact among these Thai schools was considerably greater.

In looking at each of the Lop'buri images we have thus far examined (figs. 1, 3, 5), it would seem that none displays predominantly Mon characteristics. The double-sided shrine (figs. 3, 4), however, exhibits many features that are, for the most part, Khmer in origin. We have not only mentioned the "Khmerized" proportions of this Buddha figure, but we have also commented on the effusive use of various Khmer decorative elements. It would thus seem reasonable to assume that this bronze was created sometime between the eleventh and early thirteenth centuries. The Museum's altarpiece (fig. 1), although displaying certain Khmer decorative motifs and reflecting remnants of the squared features of the Khmer figure type, exhibits some U'Tong influences in the proportioning and modeling of the Buddha image. This shrine should therefore date from the early thirteenth century, a date corresponding with the latter part of the Khmer occupation of Lop'buri (ca. 1097-1220) or the early part of the Sukodhai kingdom (ca. 1220-1349). The third Lop'buri altarpiece we have examined (fig. 5) in comparison with the other two exhibits a much greater affinity with the school of U'Tong, especially in its proportions. While this Lop'buri artist has incorporated certain Khmer decorative elements into the design of this shrine, their use is much more restrained. It would therefore seem reasonable to assign to this shrine a late thirteenth- or early fourteenth-century date, corresponding to the decline of the Sukodhai empire and the rise of that of Ayudhyā.

9.
Māradharṣaṇa Scene
Bihar or Bengal, 10th century
Grey schist
h: 20½ in. (52.1 cm.)
Los Angeles County Museum of Art
Gift of Mr. and Mrs. Paul E. Manheim

Notes

I would like to express my gratitude and appreciation to Dr. Pratapaditya Pal, without whose helpful suggestions and untiring patience this article would never have come to fruition.

1.
This bronze may have originally had still another separately cast piece—an intricately designed tree not unlike that which appears in fig. 5. This tree would have crowned the whole altarpiece and would have been attached to the reverse of the flame-bordered aureole in much the same way as that of the Pan-Asian altarpiece (fig. 5).

2.
The curious appearance of the five circles which have been incised beneath each of the separate lobes of this architectural form is difficult to explain. Dr. Pal has suggested that they may, in fact, be an abstraction of certain Indian foliate motifs. Similar circular forms have been incorporated into the design of the Bodhi tree of a tenth-century bronze from Nagapattinam which is housed in the Government Museum in Madras. *The Way of the Buddha* (Delhi: Publications Division, Ministry of Information and Broadcasting, Government of India, n.d.), 194, pl. 14.

3.
6 Soi Kasemon II: An Illustrated Survey of the Bangkok Home of James H. W. Thompson, rev. 2nd ed., n.p., 1962, 55.

4.
Lawrence Palmer Briggs, *The Ancient Khmer Empire* (Philadelphia: The American Philosophical Society, 1951), 159-68.

5.
George Coedes, *The Making of Southeast Asia* (Berkeley and Los Angeles: University of California Press, 1969), 190-91. The Thai of the Sukodhai kingdom were known to their neighbors as Syam. And it is for this reason that modern day Thailand had come to be known as Siam. The name was officially changed to "Thailand" in 1939 by Prime Minister Pibun.

6.
There is another such shrine housed in the Freer Gallery of Art in Washington, D.C., which is cast in four parts. The Buddha figure of this altarpiece displays *dhyānamudrā* and is both crowned and regally attired. Sherman E. Lee, "A Cambodian Bronze Hoard," *Art in America,* vol. 31, no. 2, April 1943.

7.
Although textual accounts of the Buddha's fast make specific mention of the various trees beneath which the Buddha meditated, it does not appear that artists, in their depictions of the various incidents from the fast, made any attempt to differentiate between the species of these individual trees. Instead, it seems that all of these trees were probably regarded as the Bodhi tree, the tree under which the Buddha sat during the last week of this fast. Thus, it is likely that even the tree of the Māradharṣaṇa incident can be regarded as the Bodhi tree.

8.
It is of some interest to note that those that are crowned display an elaborate tiara which seems to derive from Pāla or Burmese prototypes. See fig. 3. For a similarly crowned Lop'buri Buddha figure see Theodore Bowie, ed., *The Sculpture of Thailand* (New York: The Asia Society, Inc., 1972), no. 41. Like the Pan-Asian Buddha, this bronze may have originally formed the central image of a similarly designed altarpiece.

9.
For similarly crowned Burmese Buddha figures see Gordon Luce, *Old Burma—Early Pagán* (Locust Valley, New York: J. J. Augustin Publisher, 1970), vol. 3, pls. 400, 401.

10.
We see such elements in the sculptural tradition of the Pāla school as well as in that of Burma. Of particular interest is the fact that the *makara* arcatures of Pāla images and Pāla-inspired Burmese sculptures depict avian interpretations of the typical *makaras,* not unlike those that appear in the Los Angeles shrine. Also noteworthy is the polylobed arch that has been incorporated into both the Los Angeles and double-sided Pan-Asian shrines (figs. 1, 3, 4). Although this particular architectural form is reminiscent of the curvilinear forms of Khmer *makara toraṇa,* its incorporation into such Lop'buri altarpieces was similarly also the result of either Pāla and/or Burmese influences, as is evidenced by the Pāla piece included here (fig. 9). For further examples of the Pāla use of such motifs see *The Way of the Buddha,* chap. V, pls. I, II, IX, X and Rakhl Das Banerji, *The East Indian School of Medieval Sculpture* (Delhi: Manager of Publications), Archaeological Survey of India, vol. 47, 1933, pt. 2, pls. LXVII a-c, XXXIX d, II a, c, XX a.